SEARCH THE SCRIPTURES

For the Words of Wisdom found therein

VOLUME ONE
OUT OF THE DARKNESS

BENJAMIN BARUCH

SEARCH THE SCRIPTURES

Volume One
OUT OF THE DARKNESS
Benjamin Baruch

First Edition   March 12th, 2015

ISBN-13: 978-0692410042   ISBN-10: 0692410042

Underlining and other emphasis within the Scripture is the author's own. The author has translated certain scripture references into modern English for the benefit of the reader.

Look for the author's first book, **The Day of the LORD is at Hand, Seventh Edition** for insight into the prophetic writings, and for understanding of what is coming upon America and her church.

You may find other teaching materials & resources by Benjamin Baruch at: www.BenjaminBaruch.com

Dedication

I wish to dedicate this first volume of *Search the Scriptures, Out of the Darkness* to the remnant.

"The remnant shall return, even the remnant of Jacob, unto the mighty God. Except the LORD of hosts had left unto us a very small remnant, we would have been as Sodom, and we should have been like unto Gomorrah. For though thy people Israel be as the sand of the sea, yet only a remnant of them shall return: for the consumption decreed shall overflow with righteousness. For the Lord God of hosts shall make a consumption even determined, in the midst of all the land." Isaiah 10:21-23

"But thou, Bethlehem Ephratah, though thou be little among the thousands of Judah, yet out of thee shall he come forth unto me that is to be ruler in Israel; whose goings forth have been from of old, from everlasting. Therefore will he give them up, until the time that she which travails hath brought forth: then the remnant of his brethren shall return unto the children of Israel; and he shall stand and feed in the strength of the LORD, in the majesty of the name of the LORD his God; and they shall abide: for now shall he be great unto the ends of the earth." Micah 5:2-4

SEARCH THE SCRIPTURES
Volume One:
OUT OF THE DARKNESS

TABLE OF CONTENTS

REGISTER THIS BOOK FOR MORE CONTENT AT:

WWW.BENJAMINBARUCH.COM

(Audio's, Special Report's, etc.)

Matters of the Heart

"From the days of John the Baptist until now the kingdom of heaven suffers violence, and the violent take it by force. For all the prophets and the law prophesied until John. And if you will receive it, this is Elijah, who was to come and he that hath ears to hear, let him hear." Jesus Christ - Matthew 11:12-15

We are in a spiritual battle and this battle is not won by the faint hearted or by people who make a partial or part-time spiritual commitment. Our commitment to the Lord must be with the total commitment of our hearts.

We also cannot be divided and we cannot serve two masters. We cannot have our hearts invested in the world and our hearts invested in the kingdom of God. It does not work. If you try to serve two masters, you will love one and despise the other, or you will have a war within your person. Your flesh will be in love with the world, while your spirit will be grieving and crying out for God's deliverance. It is a woeful state to be double minded within your heart and to be part of the mixed multitude that gathers in the outer court.

We know from Scripture that the mixed multitude will not enter in to the promises of God or to the Promised Land. We must do whatever we can to overcome the issues of self, which have left so many of us trapped in this desolate place which the Scriptures call the flesh. Yet this is the reality in much of the church today, for many people are still wandering in the wilderness of sin, or altogether deceived and only imaging they have been born again.

We are a generation that is pure in our own eyes, but has not yet been washed from our sin. We live among the generation which has been appointed and raised up for the wrath of God to be poured out. The Scriptures refer to our generation as *"the generation of His wrath."* The prophet Jeremiah declared: "Cut off thine hair, O Jerusalem, and cast it away, and take up a lamentation on the high places; for the Lord has rejected and forsaken the generation of his wrath."[1] The generation of God's wrath is like unto the generation in the days of Noah, and the people are like unto the people of Sodom and Gomorrah. Ours is the time, and we are the nation that has embraced evil and now calls it good.

A COVENANT OF DEATH

Like Judah in the days of Jeremiah, we have chosen the lie for a covering. Our nation has made a covenant with death, and with hell we are now in agreement as a people. Having chosen a covenant of death, we shall soon discover that it will not cover us in what is coming upon our land, for a time of woe will soon be visited upon the many.

A time of woe is coming upon the people of this world and upon the people of this nation; a great woe is about to come upon us all. In the heart of this wicked generation, even in the assembly of those who call themselves saints, we find widespread compromise and hypocrisy. We have become a nation of people who cry out *"Lord, Lord"* but many do not know him, for they only know his name.

They are spiritually blind so they cannot see the truth. Their ears are deaf for they cannot bear to hear the truth. The eyes of this people are blinded and their hearts have become hardened in pride, and they do not know that they are the apostate church, and this apostasy is everywhere. A great apostasy was prophesied to come in like a flood in the last days, and because the wickedness has greatly increased, the love of many has also grown very cold.

The Scripture speaks of our time in the book of Micah: "The best of them is a thorn hedge, and the most upright among them is sharper than a briar."[2] The spiritual blindness of this present hour has enabled the apostasy within the church to grow and flourish, and because of the evil which is set before our eyes every day, this apostasy has touched virtually every one of us.

The Lord always preserves a holy remnant and he is purifying a holy remnant even now, but we live in the midst of a rebellious people. And we live in the midst of a most rebellious church. Much of the church that was called by his name has been swept away in the tide of false prophets and false doctrines. They have been swept away by doctrines of devils and they have been swept away by a false anointing, for there is a lying spirit at work in the majority of the assemblies that gather together in the name of Jesus in this hour.

They teach doctrines of demons from the pulpits, and they speak prophetic words from the throne of hell, and a false anointing which mimics the work of the Holy Spirit is now being poured out in many churches, that at one time, were spirit filled. Today in many congregations there is another spirit at work, and it is coming forth from out of hell itself, for this entire apostasy has come forth from out of the mouth of the dragon.

A STRONG DELUSION HAS BEEN CAST DOWN

Our nation has been turned over to darkness and now embraces the lie as if it were the truth. Absolute deceit occurs every day within the corridors of power inside our government, and inside the corporate world. Every part of our society has been utterly corrupted and in this corruption, the destructive forces of sin and death have affected all of us. This is all part of the strong delusion that God has cast down upon the nations who refuse to hear him.

In the late 1970's the Lord sent me to a large Christian church, which had witnessed powerful moves of the Holy Spirit. I went to one of the youth concerts, and there a Christian rock band was playing. As soon as the music started, I saw thousands of devils fly up out of the stage, and I could see them with my eyes. They flew in a circular pattern over the congregation as a cloud; they formed a canopy of darkness over the unsuspecting church.

I had spent the previous three days in the Holy of Holies with the Lord, in the most amazing time of my life in which the Lord spoke to me audibly the entire time. At the end of this time, the Lord said to me "I want you to pray that I remove my anointing from you for I am sending you back to my church, and they cannot receive you in my presence." When I returned home, the Lord told me "I want you to go to the concert at church tonight." It was there, that I saw these devils come into the church through the worship, for it was false worship, and it brought another type of fire into the church, a fire which was not of the Lord. This worship was of the flesh, born out of a spirit of rebellion and it was full of sin within though it came in Jesus' name.

MANY WILL COME IN MY NAME AND DECEIVE MANY

The Scriptures warned us that such a time would come, when many deceivers would come in Jesus name, and would deceive the *many*, so why should we marvel that this deception would come first as false worship, for Satan himself has always appeared as an angel of light and so do his ministers within our time.

Had I approached the leadership of that church after that demonic Christian concert, or had I talked to that Christian band that played the satanic music within the church, I daresay they would have not received my report. I had no direction at all from the Lord to say anything to the leadership of that church or to the musicians that were carrying the false fire. It never even occurred to me to say a single word. This was false worship; it was worldly, sensuous, rebellious, and prideful and in truth only demonic. But I knew in my heart, the people involved would hear nothing from me. They had already chosen the way which seemed right in their eyes, and no one would tell them otherwise.

This was not the worship of the Lord; it was the worship of the beast. When ancient Israel fell into the worship of Ba'al (and the word means Lord), they were, in their own minds, still serving God. But they had incorporated the paganism of the cultures around them into their lives and it had contaminated their hearts, such that they were no longer walking with the Lord with a perfect heart and as a result, they quickly strayed entirely, to where they were no longer walking with the Lord at all.

These lying spirits came within the church but the church could not discern the true from the false. Why was the church unable to discern the difference between the satanic and the holy? It was because of the matters of the heart, for the people had fallen from their first love, and they had fallen from the purity of heart that is required if you are going to actually walk with the Lord.

The Scripture declares of this hour, "The people honor me with their lips, but their hearts are far from me." If all we have is an outward form of worship, an outward form of preaching, and an outward form of religion, but within our hearts, we hide the matters of sin and compromise, then we are nothing more than modern-day Pharisees who appeared pious on the outside but in their hearts, were only full of wickedness. They had true religious doctrine, yet they were full of pride, and therefore they were full of all manner of evil as well. The Lord referred to them as "sons of Satan" and he said to them "you are the children of your father the devil."

THE HEART IS DECEITFUL ABOVE ALL THINGS

The righteousness of the Kingdom of God pertains to the matters of the heart, for only the pure in heart shall see God, but the heart of man is deceitfully wicked, so how can we know the matters of the heart within ourselves? The Scripture declares "the heart is deceitful above all things, and desperately wicked: who can know it?"[3] Being deceitfully wicked, our hearts naturally hide our sin deep within, hiding it even from ourselves. We not only deceive our neighbors and our friends with our sin, we deceive ourselves as well, for the human heart is deceitfully wicked, so who can know it?

Apart from the discerning and searching work of the Holy Spirit, we are unable to actually know what is in our own hearts. But it matters what is in our hearts, for within the matters of the heart are the issues of life within all of us. It is good to know the times we are living in, and the Lord has raised up many watchmen to warn us of the times which have come. And it is good to be able to understand all prophecy and to know the lateness of the hour, and to prepare. It is good if you can hear the sound of the trumpet and if you respond, but the primary issue that we have got to get right, is our heart relationship with the Lord, and our relationship with the Lord is totally dependent on the matters within our heart.

And that is one area where it is very easy to be wrong. It is easy to make a mistake in the matters of the heart. As a matter of fact, it is the most natural thing to do, for to be deceived in the heart is the nature of man. The heart of man is deceitfully wicked above all things, and as a result, is unable to discern its own true motives and is unable to see the secret sins hidden within.

That is precisely what is going on in many churches today, and it is terrifying, for a strong delusion has come down upon the whole earth, and *many* within the church have left the Lord and they do not even know it. This great delusion will ultimately culminate in the total deception of the planet. Difficult as it may be to believe, there will be large numbers of people, who profess today to be Christian, who will ultimately follow the beast. They will be totally deceived by what is coming, fooled by the lying signs and wonders of the false prophet, and they will follow the beast thinking they are following the Lord.

MANY ONLY KNOW HIS NAME

This is possible because many possess only a form of godliness, but they do not have a relationship with Jesus Christ. They do not know him, they only know his name. They do not walk in his ways; rather they are walking in the imagination of their own mind. They only imagine that they are walking with the Lord; and they believe they are prepared for what is coming, and they are not.

They have wandered so far away from the truth, that all they have left is a vague form of Christianity mixed in with some version of a *Power of Positive Thinking* message, where all they seek after is their best life now, and where everything is only positive. There is no deep repentance from sin, no flesh to overcome, and no cross to bear, only an outward form of religion. And there is no fear of God in the land, for they have only learned the doctrines of men. "This people draws nigh unto me with their mouth, and honors me with their lips; but their heart is far from me. But in vain they do worship me, teaching for doctrines the commandments of men." [4]

Much of Christian television today is formatted similar to secular infomercials, where the gospel has been turned into a motivational network. The liars and the merchants from Shinar have come in and turned the gospel of Jesus Christ into a business. Many so called ministries are simply merchandising the truth and the people as well. The people, because their hearts are now hardened, are buying it, for they lack the discernment to see, none of this is of the Lord.

They do not know the Scriptures either. We were instructed to study the word of God, but most people did not pay attention, and read the word casually if at all. They did not carefully study as we were commanded. And for the most part the church is not praying either, and almost no one is fasting and praying as the Lord has commanded. They are not studying Scripture, therefore their hearts have become hardened, and in the hardening of their hearts, their eyes have become dim, so that now they are blind, and their ears have become deaf, so they no longer can hear what the Spirit of God is speaking to the remnant that are being called out of this present darkness.

THE CHURCH FROM SHINAR

The many who no longer can hear the voice of the Lord are left to grope around in the dark, looking for spiritual truth, and they run into the merchants of Ba'al, and to the churches which were built in Shinar, where they are merchandising the people, counting them as "giving units" while selling them only poison. They traded their birthright in the kingdom for a bowl of cheap pottage, and a promise of cheap grace which can only be knitted together within the garments of a counterfeit salvation.

Now everything about them is only a cheap imitation, but they do not even notice the fraud, because in the hearts of the many, their love has grown cold. They cannot hear the Lord either, nor can they see the grave danger at the end of the wide road on which they travel, but they comfort themselves with their numbers, for many walk with them down the wide road to destruction. They are the many who are only religious, while only a remnant are truly righteous; for only a remnant is being saved, while the majority are passing on to perdition.

THE REMNANT SHALL BE VERY SMALL

"Except the LORD of hosts had left unto us a very small remnant, we would have been as Sodom, and we should have been like unto Gomorrah."[5] The word for *small* [6] in this verse is מעט, *me'at*, which means very few, very small and a very little number. "For though thy people Israel be as the sand of the sea, yet only a remnant of them shall return: for the consumption decreed shall overflow with righteousness. For the Lord God of hosts shall make a consumption even determined, in the midst of all the land."[7]

The word for *consumption* in this verse is כלה, *kalah*[8], and it means a complete destruction, to be utterly consumed, and a full and utter riddance unto the end. This is the word of God for our time, and this is the truth, for the word of God declares an utter and total destruction is coming. It will sweep away both our nation, and the apostate church which is going straight into hell. And the only thing that separates the remnant who are being saved from the wicked who are all perishing are the matters of the heart, for the true Kingdom of God is first all about the matters of the heart.

PRIDE IS AN ABOMINATION BEFORE THE LORD

The central deception within the hearts of the many who are being deceived is pride. Pride is an abomination in the eyes of the Lord. If you search out the Scriptures, the Lord lists those things which are an abomination to him, and the word for *abomination* is תועבה , *Toa'baw*[9] and it means something which is morally disgusting, abhorrent, horrible and idolatrous, something that is abominable and hideous to the Lord.

This is beyond just sin; this is something that is so outrageous in the eyes of God that he calls it an abomination and pride is on top of the list. It is one of the six abominations mentioned in scripture. The Lord speaks of pride, lying, deception, hands that shed innocent blood, the killing of innocent children, a heart that devises wicked imaginations, wicked and evil thoughts, people that are swift in running to mischief, false witnesses that speak lies, and those that sow discord among the brethren, the slanderer, the gossip and the backbiters. Notice that pride and slander are on the same list with murdering innocent children; these are all abominations in the eyes of the Lord.

All of the sons of pride are in reality sons of Satan. The Lord says "I will look unto those who are humble and to him who is of a contrite heart." It is through the sin of pride that the damning deceptions come, for pride is the strongman of Satan's deception arsenal against you. It is through pride that you cannot see your own sin and it is through pride, that you will not hear a word of correction from the Lord, because you already know that what you are doing is right, in your eyes.

It is through pride that you take and give the spirit of offense when somebody says a word to you, a single word that offends. It is your pride within that causes you to become bitter and break relationships and it stirs up every evil work. All of this comes through pride, for pride is an absolute deception within the hearts of men. The Lord looks upon the meek and the lowly in heart and he draws close to the brokenhearted, but he knows the proud from only far off. "Though the LORD be high, yet hath he respect unto the lowly: but the proud he knows afar off." [10]

The sons of pride all walk within the deception of the fallen nature, and they are all bound and captured by the sin of rebellion, for pride hidden within is rebellion in the eyes of the Lord. The number one thing we need to search out in our hearts, and prayerfully pray out of our lives is the spirit of pride and rebellion, because it contaminates and hardens our hearts and once our hearts become lifted up with pride, which was the very first sin that brought Lucifer down to hell, we open ourselves to the all of the deceptions of the enemy.

Lucifer was absolutely perfect when he was created to be the worship leader in heaven until pride was found within him, and then it began to corrupt his whole nature. He was the most magnificent of all the created beings, but one day pride was found within him, and his pride became a cancer within his heart, and it quickly corrupted and turned his entire nature into evil.

Pride makes us into Pharisees and into hardhearted people who are left wide open to deception, where we cannot see our own sin much less the false doctrines and lying spirits in the people around us. We also cannot see the snares and the traps of the enemy, because our pride has blinded us. All sin will blind you and the most powerful sin of all is the sin of pride and yet that is the culture we live in.

We were all taught that we should be proud to be an American! Go back and read the early writings of the Christians that founded our nation, they were not proud to be an American. They were humbled to be a Christian. They humbled themselves and they cried out for mercy and for the help of heaven; there was no pride in the roots of our country, in its beginnings. They were a humble people that were seeking God's favor and that knew they were totally dependent on the Lord. Look at the songs from that era: The Battle Hymn of the Republic. My eyes have seen the pride of the Great American dream? No! My eyes have seen the glory of the coming of the Lord! Their whole focus was on the Lord, and the love that was in their hearts was for the truth of God, but this country has been turned completely upside down. The truth has been thrown in the street and the lie and idolatry have been lifted up and sold to the people as our heritage.

THOU MOST PROUD AMONG THE NATIONS

The number one thing sold to the American people is pride. *"Oh most proud among the nations"* the Scripture declares, for our nation is described in the word of God as the *most proud* and it is precisely because we think we are number one. And does that not accurately reflect our attitude here in America? We know we are number one, the greatest nation in the history of the earth, and our pride has come to the full before our fall.

"Behold, I am against thee, O thou most proud, saith the Lord GOD of hosts: for thy day is come, and the time that I will visit thee. And the most proud nation shall stumble and fall and none shall raise him up: and I will kindle a fire in his cities, and it shall devour all round about him."[11]

Pride comes before a fall; for once you have been overcome by pride, the only thing left is to learn from your fall. You now must be judged, because pride actually hardens the heart, and it turns you over to every other false work. When you are proud, you will begin to judge, in a condemning way, your neighbor's sin, all the while, seeing virtually none of your own.

A few years back, I was in a solemn assembly with a group of people and we had been fasting and praying all day. At the end of the day I went back to my hotel room and the Lord said "turn on the television." Normally the Lord would say "turn off the television" and that is a good general rule, but this time the Lord said "turn on the television" so I did. The channel was turned to a news program showing pictures from a nightclub which had burned in Boston. As it happened, the nightclub started on fire, and the people panicked, and as they attempted to flee the building, they had literally fallen into a huge pile in the doorway. All you could see was people, lying one on top of another, piled from the bottom of the floor to the top of the door. It was all heads and arms sticking out of the burning building, but they were so trampled together, that the fire department could not pull the people out of that pile, for they were all crammed together in a big tangled up mess.

There must have been fifty people lying on top of each other in that doorway, their heads and arms were outside in the cold evening air, while their legs and their feet were still inside the burning building. And they could not move. I watched this scene in utter amazement, and then Lord said to me "This is a picture of my people, who having laid stumbling blocks, one before another, have all fallen to the ground."

I learned later that the people in that pile all burned to death that night, their legs and their feet had exploded in flames. I had watched their faces before they burned, and some of them were smiling, embarrassed by the fact they had all trampled each other. They assumed they would be rescued, for the fire department was there, trying to pull them out of the fire, but they never were rescued, and they all died in the flames. "This is a picture of my people, who having laid stumbling blocks, one before another, have all fallen to the ground." And the building we have all fallen within, soon it too will be burning to the ground.

In our pride, we judge our neighbor, we argue with one another, and we are harsh. The Scripture tells us were supposed come to one another with the love and mercy of God, but we do not come with living water, and with the living bread and with healing hands and with the love of Jesus Christ; instead we come in our pride, and with a harshness, and an attitude that says *I know* and all of this only creates division.

And the spirit of pride is so quick to take offense. You say one wrong word, one misunderstanding, one moment of hurt feelings, and the harshest judgments come down. Fellowships are broken, relationships destroyed, families break apart, and in those hurtful moments, stumbling blocks are cast before the people. We throw such stumbling blocks in the paths of our brothers, and then judge them when they fall.

When the truth is finally known, many of us will find out we were the ones who put the stones in our brother's path in the first place. The Scripture teaches us that if we see a brother in a fault, those among us that are spiritual should go and restore such a one. But you do not see that anymore. There are not very many people, who when they see a brother stumbling in a sin area, will humbly go and restore such a one. No. They will cast you out, and then slander you. They will come against you and judge you and, in this way we all judge each other. In our pride, we become offended; we create all kinds of divisions, and end up resenting each other. And Satan loves it this way.

People even argue about what language we should be praying in, and get outraged with each other over which culture is the most righteous one. But God is not testing our vocabulary, and he is not giving us a language test, he is testing our hearts. And it is in this area so many of us are utterly failing, for it is the matters of the heart that actually matter the most to God.

THE KNOWLEDGE OF GOOD AND EVIL

We fell in Adam, and in that great fall, we inherited within our spiritual DNA, this sin nature which manifests itself in us through our knowledge of good and evil. Our sin operates in our mind, through the knowledge of good and evil, and it is there, that it contaminates our hearts with all forms of evil. It makes us proud, because in our knowledge of good and evil, we know we are right, and we are so sure they are not right and so we become even more proud, because now we know for certain that we are right. The other seven billion people, no, they are not right. We are the one person that has got it right. Haven't we all met these people? How many people stand up and say: I don't have it right, please pray for me. Not a one, for everybody is convinced they are right, and this is because their knowledge of good and evil tells them so. This is all part of the deception of our hearts. We always think that we are right and we believe, so much so, that we are convinced of it.

You ask the average person what they think about the Bible and Jesus and they will tell you "I'm a Christian. I am going to heaven, and I am basically a good person." They have judged themselves, through their knowledge of good and evil, and under this deception, they are in denial of their sin. Through their pride, they deceive themselves, and simply chose to believe that they are going to heaven, when most of them are not.

This nation has deceived itself in its pride; for it sees not its sin. It also knows not, that it has been weighed in the balances of God's judgment, and has been found wanting, and its judgment is about to begin. The remnant, whom the Lord is calling to come out of Babylon, and to come into the Holy Place, must first lay their pride down.

We have to be honest with ourselves and each other in the matters of the heart. We have to diligently seek the Lord, that through the power of the Holy Spirit, he would help us to search our hearts, and reveal unto us, the matters that are in our heart that we need to deal with at the cross, so that we could finally become sanctified. Because the defilements, as long as they remain within us, are the gateways for the demons, to exercise power and push the buttons in our lives, and to keep us in bondage to thought and behavioral patterns that are sinful, and operate through the many deceptions that we have allowed to remain in our lives.

WE MUST RESTORE OUR HEARTS TO PURITY

Ultimately, our deliverance comes as we allow the Lord to restore our hearts to purity. Jesus told us, that which is outside of your body cannot defile you. It is only that which comes out of your heart that can defile you. The Lord is talking about the sins which all come from within the heart, for those are the deadly sins, and they all proceed from the inside, for they come from deep within the heart of man. The things that you can put into your body do not make the list. It is the issues which come out of your heart, that defile you, yet the heart is deceitfully wicked, so how can we know it?

One of the ways our heart gets uncovered is in the furnace of affliction; God turns the heat up to show us what is inside of us. The Apostle writes "Forasmuch then as Christ hath suffered for us in the flesh, arm yourselves likewise with the same mind: for he that hath suffered in the flesh hath ceased from sin; That he no longer should live the rest of his time in the flesh to the lusts of men, but to the will of God."[12]

As Christ suffered in the flesh, we must do likewise with the same mind, for he that embraces suffering in the flesh, ceases from sin. The word for *suffer* is *pathos*[13], which means to experience passion and feeling, to suffer pain, and vexation of soul. Some of the matters of the heart can only be redeemed when we have been through the furnace of affliction and that is why God chose to put us there, so he could draw that stuff out of us. It is through the fire that God brings us into his kingdom through the process of being born again, in which the old heart, the hardened heart of the flesh which is full of pride and self-deception is put away and a new heart is given unto us. As part of that process, we have to arm ourselves with the same mind that Jesus had when he willingly endured suffering unto the death of his flesh, according to the will and purposes of God.

THE LORD CALLS US TO FASTING AND PRAYER

The most effective way you can pursue or prosecute the suffering in your flesh, in accordance with the will of God, is through fasting and prayer. Fasting requires a degree of suffering in your flesh; it is not a lot of suffering, in reality it is only a small affliction, once you repent of the gluttony, and cast that out of your life. There is a little bit of discomfort and a little bit of hunger but it is a mild affliction. The furnace is turned on low when you are fasting and praying.

It is the will of God that we live according to the leading of the Holy Spirit and that we no longer walk after the ways of the flesh. The Scripture tells us "let those that suffer according to the will of God commit the keeping of their souls to him."[14] When you are in the furnace of affliction, and the Lord is turning the heat up, or you volunteer to go into the furnace through prayer and fasting, you are suffering according to the will of God. In obeying God's commandments to fast and pray, we then are to commit the keeping of our souls to God in well doing.

The Lord taught us how to pray by example when he gave us the Lord's Prayer, and he prayed in the following manner: "Our Father, who art in heaven, your kingdom come, and your will be done, on earth and in our lives, as it is in heaven. Give us this day our daily bread and forgive us our trespasses as we forgive those who trespass against us."

THE HEART THAT IS BLINDED BY PRIDE

We all need forgiveness, but the heart that is blinded by pride will deny that it even has unforgiveness within. Oh, we forgave them, but every time we see them, we get angry all over again. Every time we think about it, we still get upset. Intellectually we may have forgiven them, but our pride will blind us to what is actually inside of us. We have to learn how to forgive from our hearts; for forgiveness is not just an intellectual act, we have to forgive from the heart. Unforgiveness is as powerful a deceiving and destructive force in our lives as pride. These are your worst enemies, for pride and an unforgiving spirit are the most dangerous adversaries you face.

Jesus said we will be forgiven as we forgive others; and the word for *forgive, aphiēmi*[15] means to forsake and to forgive, to lay it aside, and to let it go, to leave it behind, to omit it, take it off the list, put it away, and give it up. People said a hurtful word to you, a thoughtless word, and it hurt your feelings, and it offended you; let it go, forgive them, set it aside, forsake it, forget it, and forgive it. And as we forgive others, so we too will be forgiven, and to the degree that we forgive others, we too, to that same degree, will be forgiven.

Jesus continued in the Lord's Prayer "and lead us not into temptation but deliver us from evil." In order to be delivered from evil, we must be delivered from pride and then we must be delivered from the power of unforgiveness, for if we are not delivered from the sin of pride, we will not see the sin of unforgiveness within us; and if we are not delivered from unforgiveness, we will not be forgiven.

Jesus continued his teaching: "if ye forgive men their trespasses, your heavenly Father will also forgive you: But if ye forgive not men their trespasses, neither will your Father forgive your trespasses."[16] The word for *trespasses*[17] means to slip, to lapse, an unintentional error or a willful transgression, a fall, fault, offense, sin, or trespass. Think about this for a minute; how quickly can one incident, one thoughtless word, break apart relationships, separating people that were friends, dividing people that had fellowship in the Lord, and after one thoughtless word, an offense is both given and taken and relationships are broken. People struggle with forgiving one another because somebody said or did one thing which offended, and now the other party cannot forgive.

IF WE DO NOT FORGIVE, WE ARE NOT FORGIVEN

The whole struggle is over the issue of unforgiveness. How many times have you or I done something or said something that offended the Lord? How many times? Do you have any idea? I cannot count that high. The scripture says the most righteous man offends seven times a day. That is the righteous, and we all know, every one of us, has walked through seasons in our lives, when we were not even close to righteous. We cannot even count the number of times we have each asked the Lord to forgive us, and we hope that he hears our cry. Yet we struggle to forgive someone who has upset us? Someone who said or did something to offend us, and often it was only one time, and now we are offended and we hope the Lord will forgive us for the millionth sin that we have committed. We desperately need the Lord to forgive us, and the only hope we have is him forgiving us, if He does not forgive us, then we are doomed. The only hope we have is in Jesus, and there is no hope outside of his forgiveness, and the Lord is telling us, if you do not forgive the people that offended you and trespassed against you, then neither will your Father forgive you the trespasses you have committed.

Remember, that spirit of pride will deceive you, and it is so deceptive, it will deny that it even exists while dominating the whole time, and it will also deny the need to forgive anyone. The nature of pride is deception. People actually boast about how humble they are! We hide our pride and at the same time we deny we need to forgive. People will say things like "I forgive them, but I have to stand for righteousness. I have to stand by my convictions." In our self-deception, we hide the true motives of our heart within our righteous garments of the flesh. We will destroy a brother's good name, murder their reputation and hide it all behind the false pretense of asking people to pray for them. But the bottom line is this, pride is an abomination and if we do not humble ourselves and also learn to forgive from the heart, then we are not forgiven.

The issue of forgiveness is hard for some of us, because some of us have been really abused; some of us have been deeply wounded and it was a lot more than just a thoughtless word or an inconsiderate act. There has been some serious hurt handed out and if that is you, then you have to learn to pray this through in your life. If we do not pray this through, these areas of unforgiveness in our lives can become demonic strongholds, and a spirit of bitterness will take hold. In order to release that bondage, we have to learn how to fast and pray for this kind only comes out through prayer and fasting. We have to learn to fast and pray to break through the unforgiveness in our hearts, through the strongholds of pride, and to prepare our hearts to receive the healing and the salvation of the Lord.

EVERY IMAGINATION WAS ONLY EVIL CONTINUALLY

The Lord mentions the word *heart* the first time in the Scriptures in the book of Genesis: "And God saw that the wickedness of man was great in the earth, and that every imagination of the thoughts of his heart was only evil continually."[18] The word *heart*[19] in Hebrew is לֵב, *leb* which means the deepest feelings within you, the will, the intellect and the understanding, at the very center of the man; it is your attention, and your affection, and that which you set your love upon. That is your heart and our hearts must be made right.

Our ability to enter into the presence of the Lord in prayer, our ability to walk in the Spirit of the Lord throughout our day, and whether we will have the strength to stand in the coming time of testing is one hundred percent dependent on the condition of our heart. And the condition of the hearts in our generation, which the Scripture declares is liken unto the generation of Noah, is not good, for the love of the truth in the hearts of many has grown cold in this hour. As it was in the days of Noah, so it is again, for the thoughts within the heart of man are only evil once again.

The Scripture talks about the breaking up of the fallow and hardened ground in our hearts. In the modern world, men have forgotten what it means to break up the fallow ground, for we no longer work the land. Most of us have never had to deal with the hard ground to understand how much work is required to break up that hard soil. In the modern world, we have been separated from the earth. We do not know what it means to work the earth and we do not understand the power of the curse which is upon the land or what it means to bring forth bread by the sweat of your brow.

There is also a consistency required in working the land in order to keep the weeds from coming up daily. The enemy sows them daily into our lives and we must learn to break up the hard ground within our hearts and we have to do the hard work and overcome the forgiveness issue and it is not an intellectual issue; we must learn to pray this through in our hearts to the point of victory where we can finally empty them out. In order to do this, we must embrace a disciplined time of fasting and prayer in order to release all of the unforgiveness, and this is one of the most pressing needs in this hour. Only in the place of fasting and prayer, will the hard ground within our hearts be broken up, and only then can we pray this sin out of our lives so that we can forgive and release the bitterness buried within.

THE LORD IS GOING TO SAVE THE UPRIGHT IN HEART

In Psalms 7:10 we are told "my defense is of God, who saves the upright in heart." The Lord is going to save the upright in heart, those who are walking in righteousness, holiness, and purity, but he does not save the proud in heart. They must go through the fires of affliction in order to be purified of that abomination. God does not save the people who are hard hearted and are walking in blindness and rebellion after the lust of the flesh who are only imagining that they are serving the Lord. These all must go into the furnace of affliction to be purified and refined in the fire.

In Psalm 10:1, the Scripture declares: "Why do you stand far off, O Lord? And why do you hide yourself in a time of trouble." This is exactly what is happening today. We are in a time of trouble, and the Lord is standing far off from many people. I have talked with thousands, and I hear many people say: "I do not hear the Lord like I used to" or "I have never heard the Lord's voice, and I am not getting clear direction from heaven."

Why not? The heavens are silent now, and God is standing far off from many, but why? In Psalm 10:2 the Scripture describes "The wicked in his pride", for pride is the controlling spirit behind all of the wickedness in the earth. The wicked operate in pride which is an abomination to the Lord and there is nothing holy about it.

THE LORD ONLY KNOWS THE PROUD FROM FAR OFF

The Scripture tells us "Though the Lord is high, yet hath he respect unto the lowly: but the proud he knows from far off." [20]

The Lord refuses to draw near to the proud, and rather, he only knows them from far off; for the sin of pride is an abomination before him, and many there be, that are snared therein. And to the extent pride operates in us, then we have sin and compromise in our lives and it is a serious sin, for pride is an abomination within.

The Lord calls us to humble ourselves even as he humbled himself. He is the King of the universe and the creator, who owns everything; if anyone had the right to come in pride, it was Jesus, yet he says "I am humble and lowly and meek. Learn from me." Those are His ways, and the sons of pride are walking in the ways of his enemy, who is our adversary and that very pride is contaminating everything it touches and it has touched all of us in varying degrees.

Our pride must be dealt with and we must cast it out of our lives. The Lord is standing afar off waiting for his church to repent from the heart. "The wicked in his pride persecutes the poor; let them be taken in the devices they have imagined."[21] For the wicked boasts of his heart's desire, and blesses the covetous, which the Lord abhors. This is another matter of the heart which is an absolute abomination before the Lord. To covet that which belongs to another is an abomination. In our lust, we covet. Walking in the Spirit, we are content, and we rest in the peace and in the presence of the Lord, for it is the Lord who is our great reward and not the wealth of Babylon. But the wicked boasts of his heart's desire. He boasts of the things that he has achieved, the desires of his flesh, and they are the sources of his pride.

KNOWLEDGE PUFFS UP AND PRIDE DECEIVES

Knowledge puffs up and pride deceives, while only love edifies. Knowledge puts a stumbling block in the way of another. It brings rejection and brings condemnation because in the knowledge of good and evil, people think they have found the truth, but the knowledge of good and evil is a truth without love. The scripture declares that even if I do all things well, but I have not love, what do I have? Nothing. If I prophesy but have not love, I am a vain cymbal making worthless noise. If I give my body as a martyr but have not love what do I have?

Vanity of vanities. Knowledge puffs up, and pride deceives, and in our knowledge of good and evil, we pick and choose what we want to believe; perceiving ourselves as doing the work of the Lord when in fact we are sowing seeds of division among God's people. We are sowing rocks of offense and throwing stones of stumbling into the path of everyone we meet.

If you meet a believer walking in the love of God, they will not do anything other than bless you, and you will come away feeling enriched and built up in your spirit. You will feel encouraged in your faith and you will find new joy and power in the spirit and all they did was love you and bless you in Jesus name. They did not try to correct you and they did not come to argue with you; nor did they come focusing on divisive doctrines, for they have the love of God within them, and every life they touch, the life of Jesus Christ is transferred. Grace and mercy go before them, because their hearts are pure, and they are pouring out of their heart, the abundance of what is in them. But not the proud, they are full of unforgiveness, and criticism, and judgment, and their ministry is in the letter of the law and it is a letter that kills.

THE LETTER OF THE LAW ONLY KILLS

When we take the letter of God's word and we use our carnal mind which is darkened in its understanding and corrupted by our knowledge of good and evil, and then we manipulate the word of God, we can spiritually kill people with the word. In the mind of the flesh, it becomes a dangerous weapon. The Spirit gives life, but the letter of the law kills. The word of God is a two edged sword, and it can kill people if you use it wrong. So our knowledge of good and evil, our pride and our critical, judgmental attitudes and the hardness of heart are doing more damage than we know, and all the while, we are thinking we are doing what is right.

"The wicked, through the pride of his countenance, will not seek after God: God is not at all in his thoughts."[22] The wicked will not seek God, nor will the proud seek him as he requires, with a humble heart; pride keeps people from repenting for they do not even acknowledge their sin. They do not want to admit they are wrong. They do not want to acknowledge the utter wickedness that lies within each one of us, apart from the work of salvation by God.

THERE IS NO GOOD THING WITHIN THE HEART OF MAN

We have all utterly fallen. The scripture says there is "no good thing" that dwells in man apart from the work of Jesus Christ. Even that which we try to do as good, if we do it through our knowledge of good and evil and through the fallen carnal mind of the flesh, we will turn even that into evil. You may not recognize it, but I can assure you, apart from Jesus, you can do nothing. And yet we are all proud, and in the pride of our countenance, the pride that is on our face, it hardens our hearts so that we do not truly seek the Lord. Oh we might seek a religious system in our mind that we can then use to rationalize our sin, and say that we are better than 'those people' because 'our' doctrine is true. "Thank you Lord, that I am not like that publican." That was the mindset of the Pharisee, who in the hardness of his heart was full of pride. He was blind, completely and utterly and totally blind, and all the while, assured in his mind, that he was better than that other man. He was on the road to hell, while thanking God he was not like that sinner being saved by amazing grace!

"Help, Lord; for the godly man ceases; for the faithful fail from among the children of men. They speak vanity every one with his neighbor: with flattering lips and with a double heart do they speak. The Lord shall cut off *all* flattering lips and the tongue that speaks proud things"[23]

EVERY BROTHER WILL UTTERLY SUPPLANT

"Take ye heed every one of his neighbor, and trust ye not in any brother: for every brother will utterly supplant, and every neighbor will walk with slanders."[24] Scripture warns us that the time would come when the majority of the people would speak vanity, everyone to his neighbor, and with flattering lips and with a double heart, for the heart full of sin is double minded. We can have the mixture of sin in our hearts, and how we are unstable in all our ways if that be our condition.

The Lord tells us "Take my yoke upon you, and learn of me; for I am meek and lowly in heart: and ye shall find rest unto your souls."[25] Jesus Christ is not proud. He is meek. Jesus Christ is not lifted up in his knowledge of good and evil. He is lowly in his heart. He has taken the position of humility as God, as King and Creator. He has chosen meekness and humility as his way among his people and he says "take my yoke", this burden of meekness and humility, which is the opposite of pride and the opposite of the knowledge of good and evil. The meek do not walk around thinking they know everything. But if you ask most Christians, they will tell you, they know everything. Just talk to them for a few minutes, and you will figure that out. They are not meek, they are not lowly, and they do not carry the yoke of Jesus Christ. They have another yoke, and you better be careful, because they just might hit you in the head with it, or throw it in your path, and you might stumble over it.

Jesus says *"I am meek and lowly in heart and you will find rest in me."* There is no rest unto the wicked. These sin areas that we have allowed into our lives, either through deception or ignorance, or willful rebellion; they have stolen our peace. The ways of the wicked are full of anxiety and woe and in them there is no rest or peace. The way of the wicked is hard and a constant struggle. Those who surrender and submit their ways to the Father, take the lowest place as a servant; they do not exalt themselves, nor do they walk in their knowledge of good and evil, but they walk in the Holy Spirit, and so they walk in peace.

THE SOURCE OF DECEPTION WITHIN MAN

The knowledge of good and evil is the source of the deception within the heart of fallen men. We think we have knowledge, but as Paul said, we do not know as we should have known. The Lord has opened my own eyes to this in my own life, where I thought I thoroughly understood an issue, and where I thought I comprehended everything, and then God opened my eyes and I realized that I knew nothing. That which I knew, I did not know as I should have known. And this has happened in my life enough times that I now realize, apart from revelation from God, I simply do not know.

Unless the Lord reveals the truth to us, we do not see everything. Unless the Holy Spirit grants us discernment, we do not understand everything. I do not see fully into anything, and because of this fact, I will not act unless the Lord does give me discernment, and I will not go beyond the wisdom and discernment from the Holy Spirit. I no longer assume somehow my knowledge of good and evil is going to bring me revelation. The Lord would have us walk by the Holy Spirit and not by the knowledge of good and evil and in walking in His Spirit, you will find rest.

When we finally forsake our knowledge of good and evil and learn to rest and walk in the Holy Spirit rather than strive with the thoughts of the carnal mind, we will find peace for our souls. We can rest in the storm, even when it appears that the boat is sinking and everyone else is panicking, we can be resting, and sleeping even as Jesus did in the hand of the Father.

OUR FATHERS INHERITED LIES

In order to enter into the rest of the Lord, we have to change the way we are walking; we have to decide, once and for all, to leave Babylon behind. Surely our fathers inherited lies, and our fathers taught those same lies to us. We must renounce and reject the lies which we were taught by our fathers, because they walked within the carnal mind, for they knew of no other way.

In these last days, the Lord has opened the door of truth and is calling his people to come back and begin to walk again in the spirit of truth. In order to walk in the truth, we must learn to turn away from the mind of the flesh which is filled with its knowledge of good and evil, for this knowledge operating through the carnal mind of man, has never blessed anyone with life. It has never brought salvation to any man, nor has it brought healing, or deliverance from the power of sin. It also cannot receive the anointing, thus it can never break the yoke of the enemy from off of the minds of men. It cannot reach out to bring hope to the hopeless, or love or faith to anyone. Our knowledge of good and evil brings only judgment and discouragement to the people.

If we are not operating in the Holy Spirit and in love, we are actually alienating and stumbling the people around us, and most of the time we will not even know it. The Lord warned us, if we stumble even one of the little ones that believe in him, we will surely give an account. We need to walk circumspectly. Yet we are so presumptuous when filled with our pride, whereas we need to be humble, and meek and lowly in our hearts, if we want to have the life of savior within. Only that which proceeds out of the heart of man can defile him. When the apostles fed the five thousand, they understood it not, for their hearts were hardened. They could not understand what was right before their eyes. They could not perceive the spiritual things because the hardened heart can only see into the natural and it was blind to the spiritual realities of what God was doing right in their midst.

The Lord said unto them "truly has Isaiah prophesied of you hypocrites, as it is written, these people honor me with their lips, but their hearts are far from me." [26] The hearts of many are far from him, yet they honor God with their lips and they serve God in their head through their knowledge of good and evil, thinking all the while they have the true revelation of God, and they can prove it to you with their knowledge of good and evil. Many, whose hearts remained darkened within, fall into the various forms of cult deception, walking under the dominion of the lying spirits. They embrace the doctrines of demons, while they walk in rebellion and yet are confident in the faith they fashioned with their knowledge of good and evil, and do not know they are walking straight into hell itself. They will be among the many on that day who will say "Lord, Lord" who only honored him with their lips, and Jesus will say to them "you never knew me in your hearts and so I never knew you."

Our knowledge of good and evil is bankrupt; and it is altogether worthless, it is no better than the works it produces which are as filthy rags. Operating independently of the leading of the Holy Spirit is dangerous. It will lead you straight into destruction. Jesus told us: "Verily I say into you, that whosoever shall say unto this mountain, Be thou removed, and cast into the sea; and shall not doubt *in his heart*, but shall believe that those things which he saith shall come to pass; he shall have whatsoever he saith."

The issues of faith are not issues of the mind. Believing in the mind will not move the mountains, and it is not an intellectual faith that is going to save you either. You must love the Lord your God with all your heart, and with all your strength, and you must believe with your whole heart, and not just in your mind.

The many that are perishing, have only an intellectual faith. They believe in him, but they have only known his name, through their knowledge of good and evil. They only believe in him in their minds, while they do that which is right in their own eyes, for they do not know him in their hearts. In their hearts they know other gods, and these are the gods they truly love and serve.

IT SHALL BE LIKE THE DAYS OF NOAH

Our days are just like the days of Noah, when everyone followed the imaginations of their own heart, only in these last days, most people also imagine they know Jesus, when in fact, the many know him not. I have seen this first hand, in the lives of the many people who profess faith in Jesus, yet in truth, they are following and serving their flesh. Their carnal mind is their god, and in the end, it is their bellies they do serve. They do what is right in their own eyes, and through their knowledge of good and evil, they judge themselves as righteous, while they view anyone who challenges them as evil. They love to point the finger yet they themselves are full of anger and woe. And woe unto them, for they are clouds without water, blown by the east wind. These are the Pharisee's of our generation.

In their minds, they are convinced they have found the truth and it is you who are the heretic. But they are not walking in love, and they are not walking in peace; they have no forgiveness either, and they are full of pride and many of them believe they are of the remnant, because they have figured out the judgment is at hand, and so they assume they must be in the remnant. One day they will awaken to learn, they were only dreaming while they slept.

We are all asleep. The whole church is asleep. Our spirit man is slumbering. The ten virgins, they all fell asleep. Five of them were wise and they took the steps necessary to secure the oil, which is the anointing. Five were foolish. They thought their knowledge of good and evil was sufficient and they thought they had it all figured out. They were filled with pride while they trusted in their own understanding. Their faith was in the belief system which they fashioned within their own mind. The virgins all fell asleep and when you are sleeping you are unaware that your eyes are closed and you do not hear very well either. We have all been sleeping spiritually, although some of us are waking up, others are still fast asleep and the Bridegroom is about to appear.

THE JUDGMENT OF GOD IS ABOUT TO BEGIN

Much of the church cannot even hear the Lord anymore and even among those who know the lateness of the hour, most are not spiritually ready for what is about to come. The judgment of God is about to begin and the whole system is shaking and ready to fall apart, but the people presume that because they know the judgment is at hand, they are automatically in the remnant, simply because they have figured out what time it is.

But it is not the knowledge of the day of the Lord that is the issue here; it is the matters of the heart that God is going to judge in the lives of the people. God is not impressed with your knowledge of good and evil. You received this from the fall, and in fact, it is part of the sin nature within you. We operate in this knowledge through pride and through the mind of the flesh which is totally independent of the mind of Christ and if the truth be told, it does no good at all.

Operating in our lives independent of the mind of Christ is of no value to anyone. If we want to enter into the true things of the Kingdom of God, we must be led by the Spirit of God and we must be walking in the Spirit. If all you are walking in is the knowledge of good and evil, I hate to disappoint you, but you are sleeping and you are probably dreaming and when you wake up, it will be a very rude awaking indeed. For some, they will not only find out they were not in the remnant, they are going to find out they were not even in the elect, because the Lord is going to say to many "I never knew you." He warned us that, on that day, many will say "Lord, Lord." The word for *many* is *polus* in the Greek, and it means the vast majority; it is more like ninety-seven percent and not fifty-one percent. That truth should wake all of us up.

If the words of Jesus trouble you, that is a good sign and you should thank the Lord that his Holy Spirit is pricking your heart because the goats all presume they are his sheep. They presume it, because they believe it, they even go so far as to know it, for they are certain that they are his sheep. But their certainty goes only as deep as their knowledge of good and evil, for they have only been converted in their heads, while their hearts remain far from him.

In their minds they have adopted the teachings of the gospel as their own personal religion. They have made themselves a magician in their own religious circus. In their mind, they have decided that they are one of his sheep. They have no doubt at all, because they have all the confidence in the world in their knowledge of good and evil and they are sure their judgment is true.

The sheep typically are very timid and can easily become afraid that they might actually be a goat. If these words prick your heart and you fear where will you stand on that day, that is a good sign. Respond by seeking the Lord diligently in prayer and in the word with fasting, to make your election and salvation sure as the scripture instructs us. We are required to love the Lord our God, with all of our heart, not just in our mind, but also in the issues of our heart.

The sower went out to sow the seeds of life, but only some of the seed landed on good ground, representing those who have an honest and a good heart. These are they who have heard the word of truth and received it; and now they would not trade it for anything, thus they bring forth fruit with patience. It is a long process, and does not happen overnight. The word for *honest heart* translates as beautiful, good and valuable, honest, virtuous, and worthy. The elect who are pictured as the good ground have a beautiful heart. This is how the Lord describes His elect, they have a beautiful heart, and their heart is worthy of salvation for they are willing to repent, and to turn and be changed. They cry out for a new heart, for God to search their souls, and for the spirit of repentance to come upon them. They cry out day and night for deliverance from sin and iniquity. They are seeking first the kingdom and His righteousness; they hunger and thirst for it. The wicked are not so, and in their knowledge of good and evil, they presume they already have what it takes, and so they run straight into hell.

YOUR HEART WILL BE
WHERE YOUR TREASURE IS

Your heart will be where your treasure is and in the lives of the elect, the Lord becomes their treasure. Winning his love and friendship requires us to seek him, and he does hide himself for a time from His people. He wants you to find Him, but He wants to know, how badly do you really want to hear from Him? How serious are you about having a relationship with Jesus? How desperately do you want to be His friend? How far are you willing to go to find Him? He says "when you seek me with your whole heart, then you will find me." He is hiding himself until we seek Him with everything. It we have a double minded heart, we will not find Him. The Lord Jesus Christ will not be dishonored like that. The only way you will find the Lord is when you seek Him with your whole heart and half measures will avail you nothing.

The prophet Isaiah cried "Lord who believed our report and to whom has the arm of the Lord been revealed?" This prophecy was fulfilled when the people of Israel could not believe and would not receive Jesus as the Messiah. As Isaiah said "He blinded their eyes and hardened their hearts." They could not see, or understand and so they could not be converted. The word for hardened means a type of stone that has become petrified; that has been rendered stupid or callous so that they cannot respond. The people only responded in their religious knowledge of good and evil, which missed the mark by a mile. In their pride they were blinded, so that they could not see, and they could not understand, so they were not converted. They walked in hypocrisy and religiosity and therefore they were not healed. One of the signature marks of these pitiful people is that they also do not forgive and they do not forget. They are the sons and daughters of pride. In their minds they believe and are well versed in scripture, and they will tell you so, but they only respond in pride and anger if you try to confront them with the truth. They are the children of the lie and have no love of the truth within them.

The true message of scripture, which is salvation received in a repentant heart, has been obscured by the deceitfulness of sin in the lives of these blind and hardhearted ones. All they can see and perceive is understood through their knowledge of good and evil and they see nothing through their heart. The word of God does not even touch their hearts, and when the Lord says "if you do not forgive or you will not be forgiven" they consider this is an intellectual exercise. They cannot perceive the truth as a matter of the heart; for they miss that point completely.

In the Gospel of John the Lord said "Peace I leave with you, my peace I give unto you, not as the world gives. Let not your hearts be troubled neither let them be afraid." [27] When our hearts have repented, and when we are seeking the Lord with a heart that is willing to submit to the breaking up of the fallow ground, we are willing to go to any effort, no matter the cost. We are going to seek the Lord with all of our hearts, for we must find Jesus. It does not matter what it costs, it simply does not matter. We have to pay whatever price is required to find the Lord, and when He works His salvation in you, you will one day find that ultimately the price is everything. You have to lose your life to find Him. You have to pick up your cross. Our whole self-nature, which is the mind of the carnal man, is puffed up in pride from the knowledge of good and evil. That knowledge did nothing but create pride in those that are perishing; therefore that old nature has to be crucified. You have to kill it, because if you do not, it will kill you.

That old nature is trying to dominate us and if we give any ground to the flesh, it will only get worse. We have to resist the devil and only then will he flee from you. You cannot sign any covenants with death and you absolutely cannot make a peace treaty with the enemy. You must mortify the lusts of the flesh and you cannot give up any ground or you will be overrun.

SEEK THE LORD WITH ALL OF YOUR HEART

Those who have been willing to seek the Lord with all their hearts are the only ones who find him, and to them, the Lord gives his peace, which the world cannot receive. He tells them "do not let your heart be troubled." Rest in Him. Trust in Him. Believe in Him. He is the author and the finisher of our faith. God is dealing with the matters of the heart and He is calling us to deal with the matters within our hearts and these are the true issues that matter in the kingdom.

It is not about the knowledge of good and evil properly articulated in your mind, in your intellect. It is about reaching out with the love of Jesus Christ in your heart and touching the people around you and bringing them the grace and mercy and the salvation of our God and this can only come out of a pure heart. We have to ask the Lord to search our hearts, and if we find pride, we have got to repent of it, renounce it, and cast it out of our lives.

Our knowledge of good and evil can never make us clean for our hearts are deceitfully wicked, and we are unable to properly judge ourselves because our deceitful hearts will always hide our sin, and if we cannot even properly judge ourselves, how could we possibly judge our neighbor.

I GIVE YOU A NEW COMMANDMENT

The Lord never commanded us to judge each other. He said "I give you a new commandment" and he did not say I want you to judge each other, he said "love one another." It is as if we forgot that commandment. The truth is, within our knowledge of good and evil, we simply cannot love one other. My carnal mind, operating in my knowledge of good and evil, is puffed up with knowledge, and filled up with pride and it is not going to love anybody. It is a self- absorbed, loveless nature that lusts instead of loves. It fears instead of trusts, and it needs to be crucified. We have to put that old nature off. We have to recognize that we have died with Christ when He went to the cross, and when our flesh nature rears its ugly head, we must tell it to shut up and get back in the grave.

Brothers and sisters, I have reiterated this, time and again, because it is so important that you understand that in each of us, there are issues in the matters of the heart that are only going to be overcome, by the decision to fast and pray. I did not come up with this idea of fasting and praying myself, I found it in the bible. The Lord said it, and He did not suggest that we think about fasting and praying; if you search the Scriptures, you will find he commanded it.

This is his direct commandment to you and if you are not fasting and praying, then you are in disobedience to the Lord and to the express will of God as revealed within the Scriptures. You are either willfully or ignorantly disobeying at your own cost. I would remind you, you will pay the price for missing the Lord on this one, and it is a very expensive price. Fasting and prayer is not optional, it is mandatory, if you want to move forward with God now. If you want to be part of what God is about to do, you have to clean up your heart. We have to break down these strongholds if we want to enter into the latter day rain, and we have got to do our part and pick up our cross. We have to embrace the cross of Jesus Christ in our own flesh.

Peter tells us, "Forasmuch as Christ hath suffered for you." How much did Jesus suffer for us? Arm yourselves likewise with the same mind, for He that has suffered in the flesh has ceased from sin. Do you want to overcome sin, and the world, and the devil; or do you want to stay in the flesh, and in the carnal mind, wrestling with the knowledge of good and evil, attempting to be religious? The choice is ours. We have to decide who we are going to serve, and what we are going to obey: either the will of God, led by the spirit, or the lust of the flesh, led by our own mind, inciting us to do what is right in our own eyes.

FORSAKE THE WAYS OF THE FLESH

The time is already at hand for us to forsake the ways of the flesh and follow diligently the ways and direction of the Lord. Fasting and prayer is so powerful because that is how you break up the fallow ground, and how you get to the matters of the heart. Most of us are not even be aware of all of the deep issues in our hearts. There is a process whereby we repress trauma. It is called disassociation, and in severe cases, it can actually fragment the soul where there is a part of your soul that is so deeply buried, so deeply wounded, and so hurt, that you are not even consciously aware of what happened to you. You are also not conscious of the wounds you still carry inside, and in those wounds are the strongholds, and the ground that the enemy owns. Those areas must be brought to the cross. They must be brought to the Lord. The sin issues which manifest from out of those areas have to be repented of and released and prayed out of your life.

Your heart and your soul must be restored, and the Lord will heal you, when you seek him with all your heart. In the time of fasting and prayer, God is going to do the surgery to restore your heart. You will carry a little cross of fasting and prayer and God is going to do some reconstructive surgery on your heart. He is going to cut it a little, and He will pull out the roots of bitterness, and He will put in their place, seeds of righteousness. Those who are of the remnant He is calling in this hour, bare witness in the spirit, that this is what God is calling them to do. I encourage all of you to pray and ask God what He would have you to do regarding the matters of the heart for they are all that truly matters in the kingdom of God.

THE DAYS OF EASE ARE ENDING SOON

The hour is late, the country is collapsing, and that should be obvious to anyone who is awake, so we surely need to prepare. The dollar is about to collapse, the banks will fail, then the entire financial system will disintegrate, and then the real trouble comes. Suddenly there will not be any food left in the stores, there will be riots in the cities, and troops in the streets, and they may end up at your front door. And then your hour of testing will begin and we must all be ready.

We have a little time left, but these days of ease are ending soon, and we do not need more preparations in the natural, for all the preparations in the flesh are but vanity if you have not prepared in the spirit. If you have not readied your heart, you have wasted your time, and there is not much time left. This is not a prophecy, this is just reality, and the day will declare that these words are faithful and true.

There is a short period of time left to get your hearts right. I would encourage you to gather together in solemn assemblies. Start by praying and asking the Lord what to do to be part of a solemn assembly. I understand that many of you do not know where to go and you do not know what to do. Pray and ask the Lord to show you. If people would pray and ask God for his will on how to gather together in solemn assemblies as we are instructed to do by the Lord, he will arrange it for you. Solemn assembles mean times of fasting and prayer, in order to gather together to confess your sins. The model for you is in the book of Joel. Study it to find out what it means to gather in solemn assembles. This is an absolute admonition in this hour and I would take it extremely seriously, for the Day of the Lord is about to begin.

STRIVING AFTER THE WIND

All of our efforts and all of our preparations in this hour are all as vanity and striving after the wind, and there will be no profit in any of them if we are not walking in the Lord and being led by Him. None of it will matter at all. If you are not being led by the Lord in this hour, you might as well put yourself in the dumpster with all that worthless and spoiled food you collected that you are now throwing away because it has expired. The end of all flesh has come, for its time has expired too, and if you try to prepare in the flesh for the end of all flesh, you will find all of your preparations to have been utterly in vain. Friends, that is all that the knowledge of good and evil could ever do for you, for it produces only vanity.

If you are called by the Lord to prepare, then prepare. I am not in any way coming against being a Joseph and storing food. It is wisdom. What I am saying is, if you are not being directed by the Lord, what you are doing will likely all be utterly in vain. You could be preparing everything in one place and then the Lord says "It is time to move" and you are not taking anything with you. We cannot do what seems right in our own eyes because we have no idea what is coming upon us. If you are not being led by the spirit in what you are doing, then you are following Solomon's example; it was as foolish then as it is now. If you are not being led by the Lord, you are not going to last five minutes in what is coming. It all comes down to getting our hearts right with the Lord.

You should also not worry if you do not have things stored up, or if you do not have gold buried in the backyard, because our salvation and our deliverance only comes from the Lord and through the spirit. Our deliverance is of the Lord and in the end, we will find, it was all about the matters of the heart. It has nothing to do with how much silver or gold we have or do not have; either you are led by the spirit and the Lord will deliver you because you have consecrated your life unto Him or you will get purified through the fire. The Scriptures are also very clear if you seek to save your life, you are going to lose it. And if you are willing to lose your life for Jesus Christ and the Kingdom's sake, then you will save your life. Everybody is going to lose their life, so do not worry about that, it is guaranteed; you either lose your life for the kingdom, or you are going to lose your head in the flesh and there are no exceptions.

So in terms of saving your life in the flesh, do not worry about that. You can forget about that, for no one will be able to save their life in the flesh. It is not even possible. You cannot save your life, so do not even try. But what you can do, is lose your life for Jesus sake, pick up your cross, deny yourself, start fasting and praying, and ask the Lord to search your heart, and then ask God to show you the matters you need to deal with in your heart.

THE KINGDOM OF HEAVEN SUFFERS VIOLENCE

And then become violent in your heart against these sin issues. The kingdom of heaven suffers violence, and the violent take it by force. You need to learn how to violently wage spiritual warfare and do violent repentance before the Lord. It is important to be open, be brutally open and totally honest before the Lord. In the solemn assemblies the whole purpose is to gather together and repent and confess your sins one to another; not one to the church, not one to the large prayer group, but one to another. Find someone who you trust, and where you can be brutally honest.

You are only as sick as your secrets and Satan can only deceive you as far as the sins you have not confessed. It is not safe to confess your sins to the larger church. They cannot handle your sin. They cannot handle their own sin. That is why in their knowledge of good and evil they have denied their sin. They have hidden it and covered it with all kinds of religious idolatry. They do not want to hear about your sin and they do not want to see their own sin. So you confess your sins one to another.

The way of the Lord in this matter is for small groups of people, who are sincerely and wholly seeking the Lord, to gather to do business with God. It is important for everyone to come together in a time when they have been fasting before they even gather. In my experience in the solemn assemblies which I have attended, the first night there was a time of prayer and teaching from the Lord for the larger group of seven or eight people on a Friday night. The following day, the men and women were separated to pray. There is serious repentance work to be done, and the men need to repent with the men and the women need to repent with the women. The last day would bring us all back together in a time of entering into the spirit, and giving thanks to the Lord for what he had done in each of our lives. Every time I have attended a solemn assembly, all who were there said that this was the most powerful time of their life. People went to great effort and incurred great cost and expense. They fasted and prayed in seeking the Lord and they were serious.

IF MY PEOPLE HUMBLE THEMSELVES AND PRAY

When God's people humble themselves and fast and pray, and they afflict themselves and sanctify themselves to seek the Lord, He hears from heaven and He answers. If you need answers from God then you need to be fasting and praying and gathering in solemn assemblies. Or you could do what my friend did, and buy a whole container full of food which only spoiled and ended up in the trash, or you could do what I did, and do the whole Solomon thing, only to look back and wonder why did I waste so much time on so much vanity. Friends, we have to get our eyes on the bigger picture, our King is coming; the Kingdom is coming. We should all be doing something for the Lord, for he did everything for us.

Now is the time for us to ask him, what can we do for you? And the first thing you can do for the Lord is to sanctify a fast, and sanctify your temple and clean your vessel and clean your house. Make yourself ready for service to the King and then the Lord may preserve you as an instrument of His Mercy and salvation in the day of tribulation that is coming. Or you may be purified further in the fire and then He will take you into eternal glory; as the apostle Paul said, the present suffering is not worthy to be compared with the glory that is about to be revealed in us.

So Maranatha! Come Lord Jesus! We need to lift up our heads because our redemption is drawing nigh. The world has everything to fear; for the unbeliever there is no hope other than repentance and salvation in Jesus Christ. But to the saints of the Most High God, we have nothing to fear from what men could do to us. And we should not be in fear. If you are full of fear about what is coming, pray and rebuke that spirit, for that is not the spirit of God. The Scripture says that the Lord has not given us the spirit of fear, and the closer we get to Jesus and the more we learn to walk in the spirit, and turn away from that carnal mind which is under the curse of the knowledge of good and evil, the more we can become free from fear. Fear has torment, and if you are being motivated by fear you will not be motivated or directed by the Holy Spirit.

We all need to look at this fear issue, for this is another whole area of the heart that we need to deal with. Fear is an area of great bondage for many. The fear of the Lord is the beginning of wisdom, but the fear of man is a snare. The fear of the Lord is not a fear filled with terror, anxiety or stress. The fear of the world brings torment; you can't sleep, and you are anxious and there is no peace in you at all and that is not from the Lord. Get rid of that, rebuke it. Repent of it, cast it out of your life and get into the presence of the Lord. Get filled with his spirit, and experience his peace in a world that has no peace at all.

If you have got the wealth of the world, the day will come sooner or later, when you will be walking away from all of it. The circumstances of your life, or the Lord himself, will call you to walk away from all of it. The Lord may one day say to you: "Get up, we are going now and leave all that behind" and you will go off with nothing. When Jesus sent the apostles out they did not have money in their pockets. They went completely by faith. In the great tribulation, everything is going to very quickly turn into a world where you can only operate by faith because there will not be any food to buy and whatever food is left won't be for sale.

LET NOT YOUR HEARTS BE TROUBLED

We are very quickly going to become aliens on this planet, walking only by faith. So do not let it trouble you! The Lord said "let not your hearts be troubled, and do not be afraid." This is his day, he can handle this. He fed the Israelites for forty years in the wilderness and they were fine. He is going to protect his people in this hour. When the Lord showed me the judgment, I cried out and said 'Lord what must we do to be saved from this judgment?" I was actually screaming after what I saw. The Lord spoke so calmly and said, "I will protect that which is mine, and everything else will be destroyed." So that is the test: whatever belongs to Jesus is going to be protected, and everything else is going to be destroyed.

Whatever we are doing in our lives, if we are doing it through the strength of the flesh and the knowledge in our minds, it is just wood, hay and stubble, and it is going to be blown away and burned up in the fire that is coming. It will prove to be completely worthless. Whereas if we learn to walk in the spirit, and we learn to do the will of the Father, what we accomplish will have value through eternity, and there are rewards to those who do the will of God. I always used to wonder, how do these rewards work? When in truth we can do nothing apart from him, and when everything we did through the Spirit was actually done through the power of God, why do we get a reward if it was really God through us who did these things. And then one day it dawned on me, all of the rewards that we are going to get, those are the gifts that we bring to heaven to give back to the Lord, even as the twenty-four elders threw down their crowns at the feet of the lamb.

The good that we have done, we have done through him, but in being faithful to walk in his Spirit, and being obedient to walk in the will of the Father, we receive rewards, that we would have a gift to give to Jesus. You do not want to show up at the wedding feast empty-handed and bearing no gifts. So be faithful and redeem the time, for the days are evil now. And the time is coming fast, and then all of this will be in the past.

Between now and then we are going to have a little tribulation, and we have a slight affliction ahead of us. And we all have a decision to make: do we want to continue in the flesh, producing only vanity, or do we want to bear valuable fruit for eternity. If we continue in the flesh, all that we do will soon turn it into ashes; that is all that will be left of the wood, hay and stubble for it is about to be burned.

Do we want to continue in the flesh? Or do we want to begin to walk in the spirit? The Scripture tells us not to build with wood, hay and stubble because when our work is tested by fire, we will suffer a total loss. Not your salvation, for you will be saved through the fire, but you will lose everything else. How sad is that? By not mixing our faith with wisdom, knowledge and understanding, we cannot begin to build with the gold, the silver and the precious things of the kingdom to achieve something of enduring value.

It is one thing to go through this world, with nothing. It is another thing altogether to go into eternity a pauper; having accomplished nothing of value in this life and having spent all of the gifts you have received from the Lord on the pleasures of your flesh and the vanity of this present evil age.

THE CROSS OF JESUS CHRIST

God gave his salvation through the cross of Jesus Christ, and he gave us the gift of his Holy Spirit, and all of the blessings of his kingdom, to save you and to bless you. If the only fruit that comes out of your life were the things of vanity of this life, and all you succeeded in was that Jesus Christ saved you, and then you accomplished nothing because you were stuck in the mind of the flesh and the spirit of pride so blinded you that you could not even see your way out of it to repent.

So you were stuck in the flesh your entire life and you died in the flesh a carnal Christian, immature in the things of the faith, and you never grew up. You were always a baby, always self-focused, so that you never made it to maturity, and you never did anything in the kingdom of any real value. That will be fairly embarrassing for you on the last day. I would not want to be that person, and in truth, the Lord deserves more from us. He deserves much more, not that we would have some reward or that we could be some important person, because we are not. There is nothing good about us, other than what God did in us by his grace, and let us be honest, every one of us, you and me, all of us, we are all the same. And without him, we are all nothing but ashes in the wind.

All that matters is what we can do as a thank you to the Lord, for all that he has done for us. Surely we should respond in kind and do something for him. I remember when the Lord asked me to pray for the babies that were being murdered in America. I was not even walking in faith at that time and I did not even think I was a believer. I said "Lord, what do you want me to pray for, why don't you get your church to pray?" The Lord responded "I asked my church to pray and they won't pray." I then asked the Lord, "What's wrong with your church?"

PRAY FOR THE BABIES
THAT ARE BEING MURDERED

He would not tell me about the church at that time, he just said "I want you to pray." That was the 1970's, the Lord had asked the church to pray for the babies being murdered, and they did not want to do it. They ignored him. I do not know if they were too busy, or what the problem was, but the church would not pray, that is all I know. Well today babies are still being murdered in America, and now violent persecution is about to come upon the entire church in America. Now all the mothers and fathers will be looking on as their own babies are about to be murdered, and will they pray?

Today, Jesus is asking his people to pray for their own children, and are there any mothers who care? Do Christian mothers care for their babies? Do Christian fathers have any concern for their children? You may be too lazy to fast and pray for yourself, but do you have any compassion for your children? Or is the church going to just skip it again? The Lord has asked everybody to fast and pray but will we do it? Thirty some years ago the Lord said to me "I've asked my church to pray and they won't pray." That pretty much sums up how we got here today. Most of the nation is still asleep, but we are without excuse.

STUDY THE SCRIPTURES
TO SHOW YOURSELF APPROVED

These commandments are in the Scripture, and we were supposed to study the word. Some Christians even doubt that the Scriptures are the infallible word of God, inspired by the Holy Spirit, and preserved by the power of God throughout all ages, and they are surely deceived by the serpent. You also need to understand, it is not just about your life. One person sold out to the Lord, can touch all the people around them with salvation. Noah saved his entire family, and because of his faithfulness, Noah's children were saved.

Noah was a God fearing righteous man. We have got to get this correct and there is no more time to waste. This is the last time. The judgment on the church is coming quickly now. The financial crisis is going to end, and it is going to culminate in a total collapse and then the next wave of judgment which is the judgment on the people themselves will begin. This second wave of judgment will last for about a year, and then the third and final judgment will come upon this nation, and the great sword of World War III will fall upon our land and consume everything in the fires of judgment, consuming both man and beast from off the land.

Then everybody will be leaving, and our nation will be no more, and out of the ruins of the current world order and out of the ashes of America, a new world government will rise to power, and a false messiah, and the terrible image of an antichrist will be seen on this planet, and we will enter the final tribulation period of human history. Then the abomination of desolation will be set up on the Temple Mount, and the remnant will flee into the wilderness. A short time, a times, and a half of time will pass and then the Lord will come with clouds, and every eye shall see him and they also which pierced him and all of the families of the earth will wail and mourn because of him, even so, amen.

EVERYONE SHALL BE ASTONISHED

All the families of the earth will mourn, and when he breaks through those clouds, if we have not been busy with the matters of his kingdom and his business, if we have not been fasting and praying as he commanded, for the salvation of our children and our loved ones that are lost, and if we haven't been interceding for our families, that are now facing violent persecution and death, we are going to be weeping tears of shame in his presence. Every one of us will be astonished, and not one of us will have a valid answer as to why our lazy self-centered carnal souls could not get off the throne of our hearts, so that we would bend the knee and submit our lives to his cross and his sanctification.

We will be dismayed that we did not dedicate our time and the things that we were given to the purposes of his kingdom. Many of us are going to be surely ashamed that we have invested so much in the vanity of the flesh in this last hour, because we should have known better. Those of us who see this coming, we should know better. You do not want to be like Solomon who built a kingdom for his own glory in the flesh, and you do not want to invest your life in things that are going to end up in a dumpster, while you enter the kingdom with nothing. You will find out the hard way that you did it all for yourself, and you did it all according to your own understanding. You walked in the pride of this life, and you used your knowledge of good and evil to please yourself and accomplish nothing for eternity, and nothing of lasting value. Meanwhile the people around us, many of them died, and perishing, they went to hell. We are going to weep and mourn on that day when the Lord will show us the true reality of everything in our lives. I am telling you, you do not know as you should have known, and that is why you have got to learn to walk by the Spirit.

The Lord will lead you in the things you need to do, for you cannot figure it out with your knowledge of good and evil, and you will not figure it out walking after the imagination that is in your own mind. You cannot figure out what to do, you must be led by the Holy Spirit. The most important part is to learn to enter into his presence, and the only way it is through the cross, and the only way to the cross is through repentance, and the only way to true repentance is to have a broken heart.

The Scripture talks about the flesh being crucified, and that word for *flesh* means the muscle or the meat torn open with the skin torn off. There can be nothing covering what is inside of us, in our hearts, when we do business with God at the cross. You will not have fig leaves covering your sin. You are going to stand there naked; for in His presence, all of your sins are going to be exposed, and you have got to clean them out now or pay the price later.

If you try to hide anything at all, you are not going to walk away sanctified. You have to be fearless and faithful, and because the human heart is deceitfully wicked, prayer and fasting is required. You will not get this done any other way. We are facing the greatest hour of testing the earth has ever known, and if we think we are going to walk through this in our own strength, we are kidding ourselves. Is breakfast that important to you? Do you really have to feed your belly every day? Can't you find some time to fast and pray for the people around you that are dying and going to hell? Or would you rather continue to stuff that GMO garbage you call food into your mouth instead?

It makes no sense. Fasting is not that hard. We have to learn to fast and pray. If you have started fasting and praying, God bless you and strengthen you in your times of prayer. If you have not started, then begin, it's a lot easier than you think. God will strengthen you. We have to focus our hearts, focus our energy and focus the priorities of our lives on preparing spiritually for what is coming and we have to do the hard work of the matters of the heart to get ourselves ready, for the time that is coming is upon us now and behold it is come, it is nigh upon us even now.

"Summer is coming soon, tell the people to clean their hearts."

We best get busy.

Dark Counsel

Who is this that darkens counsel
by words without knowledge?
Job 38:2

A time of fear and woe is coming upon the earth in which the whole world shall become afraid and the hypocrites will suddenly become terrified. The generation of his wrath is about to be confronted with the judgment of Almighty God. "Woe unto us! For the day goes away, and the shadows of darkness are about to bow down."[28] A time of unbelievable woe will soon be revealed unto mankind. The word for *woe* in the Hebrew text is אוֹי *o-ee*[29], a time of crying, and of lamentations, of weeping and wailing, of grieving and mourning, and it is the time of the survivor's lamentation.

This time is coming upon all those who hide their counsel within the shadows in their hearts and work their works within thoughts hidden deep within the darkness. The hour that is now coming upon earth, is a time which has never been, nor shall there ever be any other likened unto it. Jesus Christ himself warned us of this time, "For then shall be great tribulation, such as was not since the beginning of the world to this time, no, nor ever shall be"[30] for then shall begin a time of woe never before seen by mankind.

MANY SHALL BE DECEIVED

The Lord gave us many warnings regarding this hour, but the first warning was the most severe, for he told us this would be a time of unprecedented deception, and a time of great delusion, in which the "many" would be deceived.

Jesus warned us "take heed that no man deceives you"[31] for the last days would be a time of unprecedented deception, in which the majority of mankind would become deceived, and in which the greatest deceptions, would come forth from within man himself, buried deep within the dark counsel of the hearts which had been hardened with sin. This is quite a time to be alive. It is time to take heed to the things that are written in the word of God, and it is also time for us to awaken from our sleep.

In the final hours before his arrest and crucifixion, the Lord asked his disciples to watch and pray with him. "Then saith he unto them, my soul is exceeding sorrowful, even unto death: tarry ye here, and watch with me."[32] The Lord pleaded with them to *watch*,[33] which means to stay awake, and to be vigilant, to awaken and to be watchful. He asked them several times to "Watch and pray, lest ye enter into temptation. The spirit truly is ready, but the flesh is weak."[34]

The word for *temptation* is *pi-ras-mos'*[35] and it means to prove yourself as a disciple, to experience and overcome evil, and adversity, and to avoid temptation in the time of trial.

And on the night in which Jesus was betrayed, he first went into the garden to pray, and he told his disciples that his heart was troubled, even exceedingly sorrowful unto death. The Lord's heart was breaking to the point of death, and he asked his disciples to watch and pray with him, before the time of his trial, and of course they all fell asleep. He woke them up and he said unto them, "could you not pray for one hour to watch with me. The flesh is weak but the spirit is willing, pray that you be strengthened in this hour." Yet again they all fell asleep. He woke them a second time and again he asked them to pray. And the third time he came and woke them again, only now he told them "sleep on now".

"And he cometh the third time, and saith unto them, Sleep on now, and take your rest: it is enough, the hour is come; behold, the Son of man is betrayed into the hands of sinners."[36]

With these words Jesus prophesied sleep would come upon his people; a sleep which he had decreed, would come upon all those who refused to watch and pray. They would all fall asleep on three levels, first in their flesh, second sleeping deep within their souls, and third, even their spirits would fall asleep in the time of the end. And so they all slept, and the disciples didn't wake up until the soldiers came to arrest Jesus.

HIS STRANGE WORK

So too in this hour, much of the church will finally wake up when they are arrested. The sleeping church will awaken to find God is doing his *strange work*, and is about to bring to pass his *strange act*. "For the Lord shall rise up as in mount Perazim, he shall be wroth as in the valley of Gibeon, that he may do his work, his strange work; and bring to pass his act, his strange act. Now therefore be ye not mockers, lest your bands be made strong: for I have heard from the Lord God of hosts a consumption, even determined upon the whole earth." [37]

The Hebrew word for *strange work* [38] in this text is זוּר, *zoor* and it means to profane, to turn aside, to go away, and do a strange thing, a strange work. And the word for *strange act* [39] is נכרי, *nok-ree'* which means an outlandish action which is foreign to God, and not part of his normal ways, for he is about to bring down persecution upon his people, in a way that can best be described as outlandish. But he must do this, for the people are lost in the dark counsel within their minds, snared within the deceptions in their hearts, and they must be brought to the place of exceeding sorrow even unto death in order to set them free.

THE PERSECUTION OF THE CHURCH

The next major event on the prophetic calendar is the persecution of the church, in which all nations will hate you on account of his name. The fact that the disciples all fell asleep before the hour of the Lord's testing is a prophetic picture of the sleep of ignorance which has come upon this last generation.

And the third time, the Lord told them to "go back to sleep" and they fell asleep completely, both in the flesh and in their minds, for their hearts and their souls also fell asleep. And in the last days, the church also fell asleep in the spirit.

The sleeping disciples in the garden are a picture of the virgins who all fall asleep before the midnight hour. They are also a picture of this last generation; a picture of us. We are asleep. We are all sleeping now for there is a part of our heart and a part of our soul that is actually asleep, and some of you are sleeping even as you are reading this book. But the Lord desires to wake up his people. He told us to watch and pray that we would be counted worthy to escape all these things. We need watch and pray, but first we need to wake up from our sleep and come out of our deceptions.

SLEEP HAS BEEN POURED OUT UPON THE NATIONS

There is a sleep that is also being poured out over our nation. The Scripture declares that the Lord has caused the leaders of our country to fall asleep. He has cast a deep sleep upon them and he has caused the people of America to fall asleep, that they would sleep a perpetual sleep. But God intends to wake up his church. He intends for us to wake up. We need to listen to his voice in this hour and we need to wake up now.

We do not want to continue to sleep with the virgins that are going to be cast out, for they are going to awaken only to find they have no oil, and that the thief in the night has come and gone having stolen away his remnant. He will have hidden them away and for the others, now the door will be closed. There is a sleep that has been poured out upon us all, and we need to awaken from this sleep.

The other morning the Lord sent an angel to awaken me. His voice was very clear, and he sang loudly in beautiful harmony declaring "O give thanks to the Lord, for he is so good, for he has shown us everything that he is about to do in the earth."

God has revealed everything he is about to do in the earth, including how the enemy has been casting sleep upon the nations and causing the church to fall asleep as well. It is in the state of sleep that the words without knowledge have been spoken into the lives of many, sowing the dark counsel of the wicked one within the minds of God's people.

"In their heat I will make their feasts, and I will make them drunken, that they may rejoice, and sleep a perpetual sleep, and not wake, saith the LORD. I will bring them down like lambs to the slaughter."[40]

THE NATION SHALL BE SURPRISED

How is America Babylon taken, and how will the praise of the whole earth be surprised, for they will not wake up until they have been arrested by God's judgment. The sleep that is being poured out upon our nation is being poured out through a variety of mediums. One of the primary weapons of the evil one is the television. If you are sitting in front of a television, you are exposing yourself to the most sophisticated propaganda technology ever created.

The electromagnetic radiation creating the appearance of motion on your television screen is flashing moving pictures before your eyes at a 60 Hz cycle, which is the same cycle our brains operate on, only the pictures and the energy you are absorbing are being syncopated, which is disrupting your normal brain waves, causing your brain patterns to change, eliminating your discernment, clouding your critical thinking and objective reasoning skills, while opening your mind for the insertion of programs, audio visual programs, propaganda programs and deception programs. The entire world has fallen under the spell of a propaganda system.

"Syncopation is a general term for a disturbance or interruption of the regular flow of rhythm: a placement of rhythmic stresses or accents where they wouldn't normally occur. Missed beat syncopation causes a physical effect in the body of the listener as their body moves to supply the missing beat. Also, complex syncopation has been used to overload the brain to induce a reaction and as a prelude to brain washing."[41]

THE WHOLE WORLD LIES
IN THE HAND OF THE EVIL ONE

The whole world lies in the hand of the evil one, and he is a liar. He never speaks the truth, for he is father of lies, and all the people of the lie are actually his children. The entire world system of this ruined age is built upon lies. Politicians are liars. Everything coming out of the world today has the lie and a propaganda message of deception woven into it. The enemy is clever and his lies readily appear to the "many" as the truth, for if it were otherwise, they would be ineffective for their intended purpose of deception.

And the stronghold of all of these deceptions, are the words of dark counsel which are buried deep within the minds of the nations as well as within the minds of the people of God. We have all been subjected to this throughout our entire lives. The dark counsel began to form within our hearts through the things we learned as a child, as we attempted to deal with the things we experienced in the world. It has become part of our reality which we have known and understood from our earliest of years.

"Then the LORD answered Job out of the whirlwind, and said who is this that darkens counsel by words without knowledge?"[42] The Lord spoke this rebuke to Job near the end of his trial. Job's friends had come unto him with the intention of encouraging him, but by the time they were through, they had judged him. Job went through a time of affliction where he experienced the outpouring of the judgment of God in his life. The Lord allowed the enemy to do the strange work of God in his life, and Job was allowed to experience the strange act of God. God actually considered Job to be the most righteous man in the earth in the ancient times.

Satan challenged the Lord on the grounds that Job's righteousness was based upon the protection provided him, and the blessings which the Lord had poured upon him. So the Lord permitted Satan to remove the blessings and ultimately to destroy everything in Job's life with the exception of taking his life itself. His health, his children, and all of his possessions were all taken and burned in the fire. And through the process Job was brought into the place of total affliction and to the bottom of the pit of despair.

WORDS WITHOUT KNOWLEDGE

If you study the Scripture you will find the words without knowledge to which God is referring were spoken by Job during the time of his affliction. What was the dark counsel for which God rebuked Job? And what are these words without knowledge which Job had spoken? If you remember, after the Lord spoke to Job, he then spoke to Job's friends and said to them, "you have not spoken of me that which is right, as my servant Job has."[43]

Job had spoken correctly about the Lord, but Job had also spoken words without knowledge which had darkened his counsel and the counsel of his friends. These were the words which Job had spoken about himself, and he first uttered them from within his wounded heart. He spoke them in his inner man and within the self-talk of his own heart and then he shared them with his friends. He had spoken correctly about the Lord, but had spoken incorrectly about everything else.

The dark counsel of words without knowledge is something all of us wrestle with. It is the doorway into our hearts through which the enemy brings his deception into our lives. It is also the place where we are going to win the battle. The Scripture tells us to take our thoughts captive to the obedience of Jesus Christ. We are told to capture our thoughts, but how do you capture a thought? What is the Scripture telling us to do?

THE EARTH IS WITHOUT FORM AND VOID

What exactly is the dark counsel that lodges within us, and what are these words without knowledge which brings the darkness within? The word for *darken* in the Scripture is חֹשֶׁךְ, *chôshek*[44] and it means to withhold the light, to cause darkness to fall, to hide the light and to bring death, ignorance and destruction. The dark counsel withholds the light of truth from our hearts. It comes from the deep darkness of a world that is without form and void. In Hebrew, the world is described by the words *Tohu* and *Bohu*, without form and void. "I beheld the earth, and, lo, it was without form, and void; and the heavens, they had no light."[45]

The word for *without form* is תֹהוּ, *Tohu*[46] and it means to lie waste, a total desolation, a worthless thing, a place of confusion, an empty place, without form, for it is a place of vanity, a wasteland and a desolate wilderness. The earth had become a desolate wilderness, and the earth was full of only confusion, for the earth had become filled with only vanity. The word for *void* is בֹהוּ, *Bohu*[47] and it means ruined, and that which has become only emptiness and destroyed. The earth had been ruined. Who is this that brings ruin, desolation, destruction and confusion by the words they choose that are without knowledge. The heavens no longer have any light, and thus there was no light upon the earth and the ground which was once blessed now lay wasted and ruined. It had become a desolation and an altogether worthless thing, a place of only confusion and vanity, and a desolate wilderness of only loneliness and pain for the earth lay totally ruined.

God said to Job, "who is this that brings only ruin and desolation, and only destruction and confusion by the words they choose, and by words that are altogether without knowledge." These words affect the counsel within our mind. Speak words without knowledge in your inner man and they will darken the counsel of your mind. And the word for *counsel* means your purpose, your plan, and the advisement of your mind; the deliberate resolve to accomplish a purpose, and the plans for your life.

Words without knowledge will bring darkness to every plan and purpose in your life. Your entire life will become darkened and ruined, bringing only confusion and vanity in all that you do. Who is this that darkens their counsel and ruins the purposes of their life, bringing only emptiness and turns their life into a desolate wilderness by the words they speak that are without knowledge.

THE POWER OF THE SPOKEN WORD

The Hebrew text for *words* is מלה, *malah* which means a spoken word; to speak as in talking; the words that are coming out your mouth and it also means the words that you speak in the inner man in your heart. These are the words that you speak to yourself, in your self-talk. It is also your testimony when you speak to other people. The word for *without* is בלי, *belie*, and it means failure, nothing but corruption and ignorance, lacking any awareness, and totally without knowledge. These words have nothing to do with true knowledge.

The word for *knowledge* is דעת, *da'ath*[48] and it means cunning, knowledge or awareness and revelation. Job had been overcome by confusion in his soul because he had been speaking words of death, doubt and unbelief in his inner man, meditating upon them in his heart and speaking them in his testimony to his friends. He spoke words that were completely without knowledge, for there was no truth to them at all. They were absolutely and utterly false and desolate, yet Job said them, because to Job, they felt real and thus, they felt like the truth.

Job was bearing witness of how he felt, but his feelings caused him to believe lies which were contrary to the word of God. If you study the book, one of the lies Job confessed in his life was that God is now my enemy and the Lord has forsaken me. None of that was true. The Lord had not forsaken Job. The Lord had declared in heaven that Job was the most righteous man on the earth. He was the one man God held in higher esteem than any other, yet Job felt he had been forsaken by God, and so he said so with his words. Then his words darkened the counsel within him, and then Job's faith began to fail him.

Job went through a serious trial. We all go through trials and there are certainly more serious trials ahead for all of us. So we have to learn to turn away from the dark counsel of this world, and stop speaking words that are without knowledge in our inner man, and out of our mouths.

These words come from our feelings during the times of affliction which all of us walk through, for the Lord afflicts his people. He wounds us. He has torn us, but he will heal us and He will cause us to recover. The Lord afflicts his people; for he chose us in a furnace of affliction. He afflicts us and he judges us for our sin, and he does so in order to purge us and to purify us within.

YOU WILL DEBATE WITH IT

"Has he smitten us, as he smote those who have smote us? Are we slain according to the slaughter of them that have slain us? In measure, when it shoots forth, you will debate with it: he stays the rough wind in the day of the east wind. By this therefore shall the iniquity of Jacob be purged; and this is all the fruit to take away his sin; when he makes all the stones of the altar as chalkstones that are beaten asunder, and the groves and images shall not stand up."[49]

The Lord is talking about the purging fires through which he afflicts his people. He has smitten us, or afflicted us. The word is נכה, *nakah*[50] and it means to wound or to punish or to give stripes, to literally strike. God has smitten us, afflicted us, but has he afflicted us as severely as he will one day afflict those that have wounded us? No, he has not. He judges the righteous but he destroys the wicked.

Are we slain according to the slaughter of those who persecute us? Does God judge us as he judges the world? No. He judges us in measure. He only afflicts us in measure. When the Lord brings his affliction upon his people, it is only in measure and he measures it out perfectly. And he does not afflict us willingly, he is only doing what is good for us, to purge and purify us. And it is always "in measure".

That word for *measure* means measured in moderation. When the Lord brings his rod of affliction in the life of every believer, and he scourges every son he receives, he does so in measure only. The Scripture admonishes us to not despise the discipline of the Lord, for he judges or scourges every child he receives. He is a good father. He disciplines us for our own good and it is always in measure. We go through these afflictions but we are not destroyed and in the end, we come out like gold.

He judges us in measure and when it shoots forth, at first we all want to debate with it. It is like an arrow; God has arrows in his quiver and he shoots them at us, and he is aiming at our hearts. When it shoots forth, you will debate with it. Look at what the Scripture is saying "you will debate with it." But the Scripture also says "he stays the rough wind in the day of the east wind." The Lord is actually holding the enemy back. The Lord puts limits on what the enemy can do in your life in these times of affliction and suffering. In our darkest of hours, things were not nearly as out of control as they seemed to us, for the Lord measured out our trials perfectly. That is good to know, because we can relax in the trials when we realize God is still in control.

The Lord has a hedge around us, and God is in complete control of the afflictions and the trials that we go through. He only lets them go so far, and they are measured out precisely. But when they shoot forth, you are going to have a debate. You will question and wrestle with it, and that is where these words of dark counsel will come in. Which is why we have to be equipped to respond according to God's will and not fall into the deception of the enemy, only to begin speaking out his words without knowledge. And believe me; we have all heard plenty of them. Some of them come out of the pulpits of America, some of them out of our own families and some of them out of our own mouth. There are plenty of words without knowledge in the air today, and we do not want them in our lives anymore. The word for *debate* means to grapple, to wrangle, to hold a controversy, to defend, to complain, to contend, to plead, to rebuke and to strive thoroughly.

DESPISE NOT THE DISCIPLINE OF THE LORD

When God brings his affliction into our lives, and we find ourselves in the furnace, our first reaction is to debate, to argue, and to try to get out of the fire and run from the pain. A lot of people are in the furnace of affliction in this hour, for the judgment of Almighty God begins first within his own house. The Lord is getting us ready for the time ahead, and though he judges us with measure and mercy, he judges us first. But in that process, you are going to be tempted to debate with the affliction. You are going to be tempted to complain and you are going to get angry. And you are not going to understand why this is happening to you.

That is what the Scripture means when it says "despise not the discipline of the Lord." As you contend, you may also try to rebuke the affliction, but in the times when God sends his fire into your life, you cannot rebuke it. If it came from the enemy, then you can rebuke it, but if the Lord sent the affliction, then you cannot rebuke it. Complaining, debating, pleading and rebuking are of no profit at all, and they are actually going to make it a whole lot worse. Why? Because if you will not receive God's correction for what it is, you won't respond correctly, and rather you will be entering into rebellion and adding sin to sin.

BY THIS SHALL THE INIQUITY OF JACOB BE PURGED

The prophet continues "By this shall the iniquity of Jacob be purged."[51] By our correct response, after the debate is over, and the people are finally responding correctly, then and only then, shall the iniquity be purged. The word for *purged* is כפר, *kaphar*,[52] which means to cover, to be cleansed, to be forgiven, and to pardon. Through this process of affliction, which brings us to true repentance and humility, God pardons us and he cleanses us. This is the fruit that God has brought forth to take away the sin of his people. When they make all the stones of their religious altars as chalk stones, which means thoroughly burned up, beaten into dust, and beaten asunder.

The groves are the images of the religious idols in your mind; they too will no longer stand up after the Lord is finished working in the lives of His people. When the people turn from the high places of religion, and worshiping God in the flesh, and with their lips while their hearts are far from him, then they will tear down all that idolatry that substituted for true repentance and righteousness before the Lord. Then and only then will they have been purged and cleansed, "yet the defensed cities shall be desolate."[53]

THE DEFENSED CITIES SHALL BE DESOLATE

If you try to defend yourself from God's judgment, you will bring desolation upon yourself like that of a wilderness, and there shall the branches be consumed. In the process of God afflicting you, he is bringing his judgments in your life through which he is judging the sin in your life. And he is bringing forth correction to uncover the attitudes and belief systems within your heart that are ungodly. The Lord wants to purge this from you. He wants those systems, whether they are religious beliefs, emotional beliefs, pride or roots of bitterness, whatever they are, He wants them purged and burned as chalk stones. And He wants the high places where we sit in our pride, torn down, and burned right out of us. He wants this stuff rooted out of us, so He can cleanse us.

If we defend ourselves in this process, we will bring nothing but desolation upon ourselves, and then "the bows thereof are withered."[54] If you wrestle with the Lord when he is brings his affliction in your life, if you debate with it, and you complain and fight against the discipline of the Lord, you are going to wither up. You need to humbly accept God's judgment for what it is; a correction and a purging to cleanse you unto righteousness so that in the morning you can be full of the living water. First must come *a time of mourning* unto true repentance, and then, the light of the morning will come which is filled with joy.

THE WOMEN SHALL COME
AND SET THEM ABLAZE

The word of God goes on to tell us that after the branches become withered, then "they shall be broken off" and "the women shall come, and set them on fire."[55] The women have their place, and all of the withered branches shall be broken off, and then the women shall come, and set them ablaze. The scripture continues declaring "this is a people with no understanding, therefore he that made them will not have mercy on them, and he the formed them will show them no favor."[56]

It is a strange work for the Lord to bring the desolation of his burning judgments into our lives, but the Lord allows us to reap the harvest of the sin which we have sown, and it is a bitter harvest indeed, and the fires, they really burn, for they are real.

We clearly do not want to be people *with no understanding*, for the lack of knowledge is the reason people perish. The people that are turned over to the judgment are first put to sleep, so that they have no understanding, and no discernment, and then they are led like lambs to the slaughter. If we want to be people of understanding, and have discernment, and if we want to know what the Lord is doing in our lives, then we must uncover these words without knowledge that have darkened our counsel.

We want that darkness out of our lives, and if we have any sense about us, we will do whatever it takes cleanse ourselves from these lies. The Lord is actually trying to lead us to the place where he causes the weary to rest, so that He can bring us times of refreshing. Yet most people will not go there, for they refuse to receive the corrections of the Lord and do not want to listen, rather they continue to choose their own way, which leads them straight into destruction.

When the Lord sends correction, they resist and argue and they fight. They do not submit to the correction of the Lord, and they refuse to enter his rest. So they perish, like the children of Israel, who died in the wilderness having never entered into the land of promise.

THE LORD IS CALLING HIS PEOPLE

The Lord is calling his people to true repentance from all dead works, but this only comes through the breaking of our hearts, so that we may enter into his perfect rest wherewith he calls the weary hearts to rest. But the people, who are hardened in their sin, do not want to hear or obey, so "the word of the Lord was unto them precept upon precept, precept upon precept; line upon line, line upon line; here a little, and there a little; that they might go, and fall backward, and be broken, and snared, and taken."[57]

If we refuse to enter into his perfect Sabbath rest; if we do not learn to rest in our salvation, and walk in his ways through the power of his spirit, which is the rest he promised us in Jesus, then we are going to fall backwards and be broken and snared and some will even be taken. God allows the breaking in our lives so that He may break off of us all of these deceptions. God's people are being snared, and they are being taken by the enemy into the wilderness of desolation, in order to bring them to the end of themselves, where they will finally be willing to repent of their pride and finally learn to walk with him in true humility and holiness.

We can be so strong-willed, and so convinced that we are right. There are seven billion people on this planet, and every one of them thinks they are right. There are three-hundred million Americans and many of them claim to be Christians. They belong to a hundred different sects and denominations including a number of satanic cults that call themselves Christian that have millions of members.

WE HAVE ALL BEEN WRONG

Most of these groups, with all of their varied opinions, and their different doctrines and teachings, came forth from the dark counsel of a fallen world. All of these sects, with all of their words without knowledge are in conflict, yet every one of them is convinced they are right. But they obviously are not all right. I am here to tell you today, they are all wrong. We are all wrong. It is only a question of the degree of error that is in our lives. In fact, the dark counsel of this world is resident within every one of us; it is only a question of degree.

If we retain the dark counsel of the carnal mind within our hearts, it will begin to dominate the seat of our wills and contaminate all of our emotions. And if we allow it to control our emotions, we will not be able to walk in the Holy Spirit. It will quench the anointing, and we will fall back into the mind of the flesh. And that is the condition of most of the church in America. The reason for the affliction from the Lord: he is going after this dark counsel; he wants the darkness out of his people. He wants to shut down these words without knowledge. The Scripture says if any man speaks, let him speak as an oracle of the Lord, and that means a perfect, infallible witness. We are not to be speaking darkness. We are not to be speaking words filled with error, lies and deceptions based upon the wisdom of this world. We also must guard our mouths, so that we do not speak words filled with death, doubt or unbelief.

But that is what we have learned; and that is what we have known. We are creatures of habit, and most are dealing with habitual emotional response systems. They exist within people that love the Lord, but they are still caught in a trap emotionally. They are unable to unpack it, and they do not know how to get out. They know they are not responding correctly. They look back and they say "Oh why did I do that" as God shows them - this is what you said, this is what you did, and in the light of his word, they can see the errors.

They repent, but do not know how to identify the false belief system that was the basis of the wrong emotional response in the first place. And so they repeat the same process, over and over again. They are trapped in the flesh, and bound up within the dark counsel of their carnal mind. We are all dealing with this to varying degrees and there is nobody that is exempt because we live in a world that is full of dark counsel. Babylon is a land of confusion and in these last days it has only gotten worse. The lie is now called the truth in so many ways, and what is perceived and believed as the wisdom of this world, in truth, is nothing more than words of dark counsel within the hearts of fallen men.

The Lord in his wisdom sends his arrows, and his afflictions, and he uses the enemy to do a work in our lives similar to the work he did in Job. The Lord allowed the enemy to do a work in the life of Job and the Lord has allowed the enemy to do a work in the life of his children. People marvel wondering why the Lord let this happen to Job yet they do not realize, God put all of us on this planet for this reason, and that is the treatment we all receive while living on the earth.

Jesus said "in the world you shall have tribulation" and the purpose of the tribulation is to purge us of the dark counsel of this present fallen age. Throughout the years of our lives, the Lord has been so patient in his love, so bountiful in his mercy and in showing each of us so much of his kindness and grace, while we were yet so toxic in our inner man, and still walking with so much of the carnal mind still alive within us. The mind of a fallen man is proud, jealous, and envious, and it is filled with fear, doubt and unbelief; it is lifted up in pride, and a willfulness to sin. The hearts of many are burdened by bitterness and un-forgiveness, full of pride, mesmerized by the lust of the eyes, and intoxicated with the pleasures of the flesh that they have become totally deceived as to their true condition.

THE MIND OF THE FLESH

The carnal mind has all the elements of this fallen world buried deep within the recesses of its memories. Much of this carnal mind is still very much alive in lives which are filled with bitter regrets, where the power of sin remains ruling as a tyrant from within. We were called to crucify our flesh, to put off the mind of the flesh, and put on the mind of Christ, but in the experience of the believer, most of the time, it is just the opposite. We are not only are stuck in the mind of the flesh, we are full of the mind of the flesh. We operate in it and that is how we respond. We react in the flesh, anytime and anywhere someone or something pushes a button in our hearts.

You could be in the word of God, or in prayer, full of peace and joy, and all it takes is one person, and it is helpful if it is a significant other, like one of your friends, family or children, and all they have to do is say or do one thing, and how fast did you come out of the anointing into anger and all of that stuff that is buried within us immediately comes out.

It is in us because of the words without knowledge which we received earlier in life. We believed them for they felt real, so they became part of our belief system. The purging's and the Lord's arrows that he is shooting are intended to kill that stuff in us. That is his target, and his goal is bringing it out. He wants us to burn that system like the chalk stones; to tear down those high places, where these words without knowledge were erected as seemingly true. And if we are honest, we must confess that many of us have not overcome these words without knowledge. This battle is still raging in the lives of many people. Just go visit an Internet forum and see how the Christians treat each other. Spend some time getting to know them and watch what happens the first time you say anything that does not line up with their belief system. Watch how fast most of them get angry, speaking the truth in anger, and breaking fellowship over a single word.

RENEW YOUR MIND WITH
THE WORD OF TRUTH

This toxic system has not been uprooted in the lives of many of God's people. And yes the demonic is involved, but even if you cast out the devil, you will still have to cleanse and renew your minds with the word of truth. And you will still need to remove that false belief system formed within your soul through the words that were without knowledge.

It is the deception where you only see the speck in your brother's eye, and then get offended and angry and judge him, only because he reminds you of the log in your own. I am not talking about false doctrines, and I am not talking about the people who are going to hell, who merely think they are Christians.

I am talking about the true church and about the dark counsel that is within each of us that causes us to wound each other, and kick our brother when he is down, and to respond with selfishness and narcissism. All of these corruptions can remain within our personality, even though we know the Lord, and even though we have correct doctrine. There are a lot of toxic believers out there, and a lot of hurting people who do not know how to let go of the dark belief systems which they call the truth.

I am talking about our emotional beliefs that cause us to react with fear or criticism, judgment and anger, or pride and envy. And where is all this coming from? It comes from the belief system that we created, and that was formed within us throughout our lives. And at one time we believed in these paradigms as if they were the truth, because they helped us. This belief system that people have formulated in their minds is contrary to the revelation of Scripture, yet it is through this system, that they first learned to understand their lives. It is how they saw the world while the veil remained over their eyes.

The dark counsel is the belief system that was formed within us, and has become a part of our personality, and it is how Satan has access to us. It is the buttons the enemy pushes to divide and conquer the church. It is the buttons they push to ruin marriages, to destroy friendships, and that cause Christians to stand up against other Christians. It is the belief system in us that causes us to be so toxic to each other.

Yet when we are operating in that dark counsel, we are so convinced that we are right, and "they" are not right. Have you ever noticed it is always the other people who have it wrong? It is never us. The dark counsel of our mind is the belief system that had its origin in the hurtful experiences of our life. We formed it to help us understand and cope with the painful experiences of this harsh world in which we lived when we were young and thus it became our truth. It is the way we understood and learned to relate to the world of the flesh, and thus we became trapped as prisoners of this dark counsel in our minds.

Throughout much of our lives it remained undisturbed in the deep recesses of our minds, buried within wounded memories, hidden even from ourselves within the deep places of our hearts. It is the belief system we learned from the world, but in reality it came straight out of hell, and it is very well organized and much defined. It was taught to us from our earliest years and we learned it well. It is how we learned to view our true self or our identity as we understood it, and how we therefore, learned to relate to the world around us.

The dark counsel within us is the core belief system of the inner man, and it is built upon a foundation of lies. Its architecture and the frame of its construction is often built with shame and rejection, fear and unbelief; while the outer façade of this fortress is covered in pride which has been tightly wrapped around our minds. This structure has landscaped gardens in our imagination that are beautiful to behold, where we seemingly enjoy the pleasures of this world, but in reality the grounds around this building are covered with only briars and thorns. And this dark counsel within us has made each of us so toxic that when it manifests, and it does, it affects everything in our life until we finally uproot it and destroy it.

THE HABITATIONS OF CRUELTY

Scripture tells us "the dark places of the earth are full of the habitations of cruelty"[58] and people who react on the basis of the dark counsel in their minds are cruel, while they stand for what is right, either their rights, or their religious views or their interpretation of the Scriptures. And they do not care who they have to hurt to prove their point, for compassion and empathy are never found coming forth from the dark places of the earth.

For them, it is all about being right. The dark places of the earth are full of things that are continuing to destroy the people of God. It is around this dark counsel that a lot of people build a religious system, which are the high places in their minds that the Lord wants broken down and burnt to the ground. These are the high places which we erect in our minds, our religious dogma and our imaginary doctrines, and we are all pretty skilled at creating a religious façade that hides the true darkness which remains in our hearts, where the old sin nature is still very much alive in our lives.

One of the central elements of this system is denial. We will tell ourselves and others that we are not proud, all the while boasting about how humble we think we are. Everything is couched in religious terms, for we are all skilled at the spin game in our own minds. When we tell our version of the truth, we are always the victim and we are always right, and we are never the person that brought the pain, we are never the one who did the wrong.

It is within this dark counsel that we do so much damage, convinced in our own minds that what we did was right. But we are totally deceived, for even though we are convinced that we are right, we could not be further from the truth. Because when you look behind these religious façades, you will find they are all just a lie. We are just hiding our old nature under a religious veneer, while it is still very much alive in our lives. If we are truly saved and we have been born again, our spirit man has come alive in Jesus Christ, but in our soul we are left with the hard work of conquering the land. We must uproot the giants from our hearts and cast out the enemy and take back the land of our mind, will and emotions, for the sake of God's kingdom. Just as Israel had to battle to take the Promised Land, we have to battle to take back our soul from these dark forces, which through dark counsel, have literally ruled over many areas of our life for all these years.

We have to uproot these giants, and in most of us, if we are honest in this hour, that work remains undone. That is why so few relationships can withstand any test of time. It is also why there so many religious deceptions and why people run after them because they are looking for a magic key. They know they are not right and they do not have the victory in the inner man. They know the torment of the dark counsel, and they see the damage it has done, for all they have to do is look at the burning bridges behind them over the course of their lives. So they know there is a problem, and they are looking for the solution. But they do not understand how to get free, so they look instead for a magic bullet, and for a secret key to unlock the power of the kingdom of God.

MANY SHALL RUN TO AND FRO

"And they shall wander from sea to sea, and from the north even to the east, they shall run to and fro to seek the word of the Lord, and shall not find it."[59]

Many people are running to and fro, searching for whatever might be the key. Should we run to Bethel? Should we look to some man? Should we learn to pray in a foreign language? Might any of that do? Hardly, the whole issue is buried within our identity, and hidden in the shadows inside of our hearts, and within the image we see when we look in the mirror. These lies are inside of who we believe we are, and what we believe we see.

I grew up on the south side of Chicago, and when I was young, it was a pretty rough place. I later moved to California, at the age of twelve, to a city called Corona del Mar, the Crown by the Sea, which was not a rough place at all. In Chicago, I learned that I needed to fight to survive, and if somebody was going to threaten or challenge me, then I needed to hit them harder or be able to run faster. And the angrier I could become, the safer I would be. If you were small, you needed to get angrier than the rest or you would get pummeled. So in my dark counsel, I believed being angry would protect me, both from my fears and my enemies, and if I got in your face and challenged you, then you could not hurt me.

That lie would cause me to respond later in life in ways which were totally incorrect. I still thought like a kid on the streets of Chicago, trying to defend myself from someone I believed was trying to kill me. I could be in a conversation with friends or family, and something would trigger me, and the next thing I know, I am responding with a belief system from the past that is totally inappropriate. That is an example of how dark counsel can become our undoing, but the darkness is buried so deep within us, within our very identity, that often times we don't even see it, and scarcely know that it is there. In my identity, I was still trapped within the mindset of a frightened child who was lost in Chicago, a place where my best friend and I got jumped while just walking home from school in the fifth grade. I was able to get away, while he got sent to the hospital for several months.

Some of us lived in some pretty scary places when we were young. Arriving home from school was sometimes even scarier for me. I wasn't quite sure whether I was safe when I got to my own house, for inside that house, danger lurked in the shadows, and you never knew when it would jump out and get you. The hardest memories for me to overcome were the ones that came out of the shadows in my own home when I was young. When a little boy is beaten with fists in his face, later in life, it can be hard for him to understand or to believe in a thing called grace. God's mercy is upon us in even our darkest times, but we cannot see that when we are hurting, and scared all the time.

These terrible times can affect your mind, altering who you believe you are, and what you perceive other people to represent as well. How we relate to other people can be completely divorced from the love of God and the fruits of the Holy Spirit. These belief systems color our emotions, they alter our behaviors, and eventually, they always come out. Oh we can try to suppress them, I would not get angry that often, but under the right circumstances, I was ready for war, and I mean the real kind. There was a rage that had been beaten into me when I was young, and I did not know how to stop myself from turning into the same monster after I grew older. This was a part of the dark counsel within my heart, and part of the dark side of my carnal identity and it was the wrong identity for a Christian.

HE IS PAYING FOR EVERYTHING NOW

Several years after I was saved, I was caught up in a vision and I was there with the Lord. The Roman soldiers were beating him with their whips. Exhausted, they finally stopped, and one of them turned to me, and hit me in the stomach with the butt of the whip. He said to me, "You want to hit someone? You have to hit him; he said he is paying for everything now, so if you want to hurt someone, you have to hurt him." I dropped the whip, and I began to cry. I had seen the Lord as they beat him, and I had watched as he prepared to die. But the pain was so hard to overcome, it took years for me to finally see just how much hatred and anger was buried within me. And it was very difficult to let go of all of the pain and anger that had been so seared into my soul that it actually had become part of me.

Later in life, the Lord came to me and I saw the Shekinah presence of God burning as golden flames of fire, and God spoke to me out the flames saying "I am going to take your entire life from you now, and you have choice, either come willingly or I will take it by force. And you think you have seen hard times, but I tell you no. You have not seen hard times, for the times which you thought were hard, I covered you with the mercies of my hand. But I will bring hard times upon you now, for I am going to take your entire life from you." While I was writing this book, I was speaking with the Lord, and I asked him: "Lord, I don't understand. How was it that you covered me with the mercies of your hand? Where was the mercy when I was being beaten in a bath tub, and I watched the waters turn red as I was knocked unconscious from fists to my head?" The Lord answered me and said: "I wouldn't let him break the bones in your face." When the Lord told me that, I realized he had been there protecting me the entire time. The bruises and the black eyes, they all heal quite fast, but the wounds in our hearts, in some of us, last for a lifetime.

Our identity is shaped by our experiences, but more precisely it is created by how we define and understand these experiences. Like the roots of a tree, which grow into the ground, this knowledge becomes embedded within us, and these wounds shape our character, and even become a part of our personality. Our memories are recorded as feelings, fear or pain, rejection or shame, or happiness and joy. But the painful memories are ten times as powerful as the happy ones, and the really traumatic ones, they can last forever, as horrors and traumas which forever remain hidden within the corridors of our minds. And some of us get lost running from these shadows, which seem to always appear, again and again, later in life, as if behind every corner. They seem to be always lurking in the darkness, only waiting for us to put our guard down, and then once again, they suddenly reappear.

THE CORE BELIEF SYSTEM WITHIN

The dark counsel is formed within these traumas, where we allow these unresolved feelings to become part of our belief systems. The lies of shame and fear, and anger and doubt or hopelessness, come in, and we begin to believe this is how the world is always going to be, and then we develop a coping mechanism, which becomes a part of our personality, which is always ready to fight off the monsters. But this dark counsel, and our readiness to fight these monsters, also creates a belief system which now begins to color our feelings, and we can begin to see the monsters everywhere we look. We know the monsters are real, because they remain alive inside of us, in the memories of how we used to feel.

Our depressions and fears, our despair and unbelief, can actually become a part of our faith, for it is in them that we were first taught to believe, and it is through them, that we learned to give and receive. These monsters can actually begin to color all that we perceive. If we are going to overcome the world, the flesh, and the devil then we must begin to overthrow this wicked system of unbelief and begin by establishing new boundaries in our lives, where the lies no longer defend us, and where our truth is no longer based upon what learned when we were young. As we discover how to set new boundaries, we can begin to reclaim our identity from these abominations within.

I am no longer that little child who was running for his life on the streets of South Chicago, scared to death the whole time, who saw every person as a threat of one sort or another. I do not have to rely on anger or intimidation to feel safe, and I don't have to run in fear, or hide anymore.

I can now begin to act within a belief system fashioned after Holy Scripture and led by the Holy Spirit. If we are going to overcome this world we must renew our minds with the true identity of who we are in Jesus, and we must place boundaries around the choices that we make, and they cannot be based on what we feel, for far too long Christians have been buffeted by what they feel. Nor can these boundaries be based on what we used to believe, nor based upon our experiences or our expectations in the world.

Everything we feel about our identity is a fruit of the memories we have stored up within. It is understood through the words we have used which express the feelings that have remained within. Our personality becomes a collage of all the words we have received and all of the things we believed, and these have influenced our thoughts and colored the choices we made in the past.

As we grow, mature, and change over life, these old memories that defined who we thought we were within our hearts can continue to influence how we perceive and what we believe about who we are today. And who we think we are is the biggest driver on how we arrive at the decisions in our lives. Who are you? At one time, this was based entirely on who we felt we were, and it was fashioned from the memories and the lies we once learned, which for a time, appeared as the truth. But as Christians, now our truth can be based on the revelation of God's word alone.

Today is the day which the Lord has made, and it is the day of our salvation. With God and his truth on our side, we can now change everything. Our salvation in Jesus is so complete that he can save us from all of our sinful thinking which comes forth from the darkness within, renewing our minds through the washing of his word to overthrow and uproot the dark counsel within, so that we can begin to operate and to act, in the power of his Holy Spirit.

These thought patterns where the enemy has had rule over us, are the high places in our minds, and where the enemy has deceived us. In my case, the deception was the belief that holding onto all of that anger and pain somehow made me safer, and thus the hurts could never happen again. And if anybody threatened me, I would just become a bigger threat to them. Well that works great on the mean streets of America, but it does not work out really well in relationships and it does not equip you to be a good Dad, or a husband who is tender and loving and kind to his wife. My dark counsel produced only disaster, ruining both my family and friendships, until I uprooted it from out of my life.

FORGIVENESS IS THE KEY

Forgiveness is the gift that allows us to let go of the pain, and all of the hurts and all of the lies that came with it. The shame and the anger, the frustration and the fear, they all disappear when we go to the cross and have enough faith to be brave and finally to tell the whole truth. The Lord will then cleanse us from all of these secret sins, and the word of God can begin the work of restoring us from within. The Lord wants to restore us totally, and that restoration requires a complete overhaul, a total repair of our vessel, removing all contraband from the inside, to finish and to bring to completion, his work of redemption, and to restore 100% of the sea-worthiness of your life.

The beginning of God's redemption starts with the renewing of our minds. The complete overhaul includes removing all wreckage, repairing all damage, and restoring to the original condition, all of the component parts of your life, back to God's original plan.

The word of God allows us to uncover the lies, so that we can hold onto the truth, and discard the belief system that is nothing more than the dark counsel from our past, and then learn to actually live in the truth. This is the heritage of the Saints of the Most High God, who walk not according to the ways of the world, or the feelings that were formed in us from the image of the world, but according to the revelation of the word of God, in the person of Jesus Christ.

AN ISSUE OF IDENTITY

The central issue in the spiritual war that is raging in the hearts and minds of the people of God today is an issue of identity. Who am I? Who is that person that you think of when you think of yourself? Through Jesus, and through faith, you are who the Lord chose you to be. And the fears that many of us battle, they exist only so you can destroy them. They are your testimony, and they are the giants in your land. These false belief systems, with their roots of bitterness, resentments, and anger, are the giants in the land that we must overcome if we are going to enter in to the Promised Land in the spirit.

A circumcision of our heart occurs, as we consciously choose to lay down the carnal mind and the heart of the flesh, and begin to walk out the will of the Father in our hearts, in ways that we have never been able to do before. The Lord tells us to love our enemies; he tells us to bless those that persecute us, and that is not an easy thing to do. It cannot be done in the mind of the flesh under the power of dark counsel. The reality is if we are living in the dark counsel of the carnal mind, it is impossible to do.

If you have an enemy who was at one time a close friend, who later betrayed you, and brought grave injury to your life. In the dark counsel of your mind, you are not going to love your enemy. You are likely to feel like doing something other than love to him. But after you have torn down the dark counsel and entered into the spirit and have the mind of Christ, you can pity the man. In truth, he is coming after God's anointed. All of these people that attack us are full of their own envy and bitterness, and they are lost in their own deceptions. If they choose to come against us, they are people to be most pitied because they are going to find out they were coming against the Lord.

PRAY FOR YOUR ENEMIES

We should pray for our enemies, but in our dark counsel, we do not want to pray for them, and we do not want to love them. We want to get as far away from them as possible, and we do not have any positive feelings for them at all. We need a circumcision in our hearts, where we cut away all of this darkness of the flesh, and cleanse our minds from all these words that are without knowledge, but to do so, we need to consciously lay down the carnal mind.

We overcome the world and the enemy through the blood of the lamb and by the word of our testimony, and our testimony needs to be the truth, not a testimony of words without knowledge. Our testimony is what we testify and bear witness of as our truth as we live our lives out, day-to-day. You will give an account of every idle word that came out of your mouth, because every word you utter is a part of your testimony. If you are speaking words without knowledge, you are going to give an account, for you are darkening not only your own counsel, but also the counsel of every person that hears you. That is why a root of bitterness defiles many. It does not just defile your life; it defiles everyone and everything you touch.

THE TRUTH SHALL SET YOUR FREE

The truth is where we start on the road to recovery. We must find the courage and the faith to come clean and tell ourselves the truth, only then can we begin to tell the truth to each other. One day we will all give an account of every idle word that came out of our mouth, and we will face everything that we have tried to hide from, and in the end, our decision to embrace the truth is the first step in our deliverance from the lie, and is the major part of our testimony. Until we are ready to tell the truth, to find the truth, and to love the truth, and only the truth, we will continue to walk in the deception and the lie of our own dark counsel.

We have to overcome the world, the devil, and our flesh by the blood of the lamb and the word of our testimony. And our testimony needs to be the truth, and not a testimony based upon our dark counsel from the past. Jesus has done his part; the blood of the lamb has been shed. And now we need to do our part. We need to sanctify the word of our testimony with the truth, and change the testimony of our lives, by living holy unto the Lord and wholly within the truth.

WE DIED IN JESUS CHRIST

And our testimony is this, that we have died, and the life of Jesus is now alive in us. We must allow the faith of Jesus Christ to begin to rise up in us. We have to choose to walk in the mind of Christ and put off the carnal mind of the dark counsel of this present wicked age. We must begin to allow the faith of Jesus Christ to rule in our hearts. This is only released through our willingness to let Jesus rule in our lives. We have to say no, and no more, to the feelings of the flesh that try to rule over us. Feelings of depression and anger, bitterness and hopelessness, pride and rebellion, they all come out of the dark counsel and they get triggered by the circumstances in our life.

In turning from the lie, we must also renounce the carnal mind of pride. We need to go back to the people we loved, whom we have hurt, and tell them the truth, for when we do, our pride dies. As we turn our hearts to the truth, we are also turning to the Lord who died for us, for he is the truth, and as Jesus now lives in us, we begin to overcome the world through our faith, hope and love. Then the truth will begin to finally set us free. This is not an easy journey, and for many of us, it is still a long road home. Negative things will happen, and the enemy will challenge our new resolve to walk in the truth, and things may get a lot worse in the flesh before they get better. But if we buy the truth, and sell it not, the Lord will keep us in perfect peace if our mind remains stayed upon him.

We need to get our mind off this system of lies, which is the dark counsel of the false satanic belief system that we inherited and nurtured throughout our lives, and begin to put to death the mind of the flesh, by learning to walk in the truth. We must strive to stay in the presence of the Spirit of God, and in the wise counsel of the word of God, and then our minds can begin to stay on the Lord. When we do, then he will keep us in perfect peace even when we are in the furnace of the tribulation.

We begin our restoration and deliverance with the *logos*, which is the written word of God; as we begin to let the word of God rule in our lives, we will begin to overcome the dark counsel, which is overturned as we allow the spirit of God to search out our hearts through the written word. As we begin to walk in the written word, in truth and in love, judging ourselves daily, then the *rhema* or the spirit breathed word begins to manifest within our hearts and minds.

WALK IN HUMILITY

In order to overcome the dark counsel of this present age, we must walk in the greatest level of humility. If we always speak the truth in love, it comes easier, for pride can only exist, hiding behind the lies we at one time called the truth. The old nature has been winning many arguments in our minds; in the past, when affliction would come, and the arrows of the Lord were shot forth, we would debate with it, and in those days the dark counsel and the devil usually won the debate.

That is why so many people are all withered and dried up spiritually, for the old man has been winning many of these arguments over the years. But God keeps bringing us back to the place of confrontation, because he wants us to uproot the sinful belief system that lies within us, which has been deceiving us all through the years.

The Lord keeps bringing us back to this place because it is the place of healing, deliverance and victory. The enemy knows his power in your life is limited and he can only operate through the points of compromise, and the places where we are captive by our fears and unbelief within this deceptive system of dark counsel which we learned to call the truth. It is a very deceptive system, and the enemy has worked so hard to propagate it throughout the church.

We have to know who we are, and who we have been called to be. We have been called to be like Jesus. And who was Jesus?

Jesus was the Son of God, and he always walked in the will of the Father, for he always spoke the truth in love. He calls us to lose our lives, as he did, if we want to find true life in him, and to lay down our self-life for the truth, if we want to find the only true life, which can only be found in him.

To lose our self-life which is bound by the curse through the power of sin, where the only fruit is death, we must learn to walk in the power of the resurrection life, which is a life that has been laid down, a life where we honor our commitments, keep our word and speak only the truth in love.

LOVE ONE ANOTHER

We are commanded to love one another and to speak the truth in love. We are commanded to pick up our cross; and we are commanded to honor our commitments to one another, and to let our yes mean yes, and our no mean no. But somehow in the dark counsel of our minds, we rationalize ways to not keep our commitments, and why we don't need to love one another, why we can keep passing by the cross and why just being religious is good enough.

The devil wants to lead all of us away from the path to the cross. He wants you to run, and take the easy way out. And he will give you plenty of reasons to justify running. He will give you lots of reasons why you should disregard God's word and do whatever feels right according to your dark counsel and these reasons feel very real for they are empowered by fear, and it is a fear that's real. We must determine in our hearts and minds that we are going to face the fear, walk in the will of the Father, and walk out God's word in our lives, and it does not matter what the consequences may be.

FACE THE FEARS

We have to face the fears that have over ruled us, and thereby ruined us. We have to overrule the identity we have known which was based upon the feelings of who we were. We must embrace who the Lord says we are in him, and we must be willing to die unconditionally to love. We have to die for one another, unconditionally, regardless of the cost, or the reaction of the people, or how much we are afraid. We have to be obedient to the Lord in this matter, regardless of our feelings. If we are not faithful in little things, why would God give us anything more?

The battle of our faith is fought over the issue of love in our life. That is the real battle, and the only one worth winning. The Master told us "they will know you are my disciples" because you argue among one another, or judge one another, and condemn one another, or was it that you love one another? This was the sign that would show the world we belong to him, that we love one another, even as he loved us. If we cannot love each other in the present hour, while we are running with the footman, how will we love one another in the days that lie ahead, when we will all be running with the horsemen of the book of Revelation?

MANY SHALL BECOME OFFENDED

In the days that are coming, when the heat is turned up, *many* shall become offended, and hate one another, and betray one another, even unto the death. And the word for *offended* in the Greek is *skandalidzo*, which means to trip up, to stumble, to fall into apostasy and to bring an offense. The word for *betray* is *paradidomee* which means to yield up, to deliver, to betray, to put in prison, and to recommend for the death, and the word for *hate* in this text is *miseho* which means to detest and to persecute.

In the days ahead, who are we going to be? Our destiny is going to be shaped by what we chose to believe, either the dark counsel of the world, or the revelation of the word of God through the power of the Holy Spirit, and we will walk in which ever truth we chose.

The dark counsel operates strictly in people who think they are right, and in the hearts of people filled with pride. It manifests in people who are deceived, who believe they are always right. That is why it is called deception. "Evil men will wax worse and worse deceiving and being deceived."[60] Even the outright evil ones, believe they are right. There are millions of people who are walking in complete wickedness, who are carrying a Bible around believing they are the most righteous person on the planet. If you talk to any of the people who have ever known them, they will tell you, "I wish I never met that person." These are very dangerous people who are so toxic, if you ever get close to them, you will get wounded, for they are sons of Belial, and you have to deal with them with spears and iron. They are walking in seriously deranged darkness, with hearts turned wholly over to evil, and yet all the while they can profess faith in Jesus' name.

LITTLE FOXES DESTROY THE GARDEN

The dark counsel in the life of true believers, allows the enemy to destroy the garden in their life. These are the little foxes that are bringing ruin to the things that should be blessed in our lives. This battle is fought over the love issues in life; yet many people have been living lives that have been defeated at the relationship level. Their relationships have been destroyed, alienated, separated, and divided.

Many people are living under the rule of spirits of fear, guilt and shame, or they are dominated by the spirits of pride and the lust of the eyes. They compensate for this darkness with a life lived by religious efforts through the power of the carnal mind, and the whole system is an abomination. The enemy desires to be lifted up in the holy place of our hearts, and it is there that he wants to rule and reign in us through these lies. We must learn to go forth from the shadows of that dark place and overcome the dark counsel, the things which we have believed that have kept us bound in fear, or lust, and advance into a place of true unity and accountability, if we are going to face and defeat these giants.

The best thing we can do is to face our fears. Acknowledge them for what they are, then place hell under our feet and begin to walk by faith. We start by honoring God, keeping his word at all cost and fearlessly facing and telling the truth. You are your word. Let God bring closure to the lies of your past, the fears and the doubts and become fearless in facing the truth.

HIDDEN IN THE DARKNESS

One of the central characteristics of the dark counsel is that it always must hide in the darkness for it cannot come out into the light. It tells you to hide your fears, hide those secret struggles, and hide those parts of your life where you cannot quite overcome. As long as we hide from the truth, we will remain defeated. In order to overcome the dark counsel, we must come out into the light. Be transparent, tell the truth, confess your sins one to another, and the Scripture is very literal here; it means precisely one to another one. Find someone you trust, that you know is a faithful friend, spouse, brother or sister in the Lord, where you can be honest, and where what you confess is not going to end up all over the Internet.

Love covers a multitude of sins; while dark counsel loves to uncover the sins of others through slander, because in the religious system of the darkened ones, if I talk about your sin, I don't need to look at mine. If I uncover your sin, maybe I can hide mine a little bit longer. Slander is one of the abominations that the Lord lists in the scripture. In the dark counsel of the religious mind, slander is one of the most common ministries of the day. Many people feel they are called to the ministry of slander which is the accusation of the saints, but they are actually ministering for Satan. Though they will tell you that they are a pastor, or an elder, a brother or sister, their actual ministry is for the spirits of evil and they came to serve their father, the devil. If you want proof of their ministry, just look at their fruit, all the wounded lives and the testimonies which they have destroyed.

BE TRANSPARENT AND CONFESS YOUR SIN

We all need to be transparent and confess our sins, but do so one to another. Confess your doubts, confess your fears, humble yourselves, face your fears, for the highest call and the purposes of God in our lives is to become a living sacrifice for the truth of his kingdom. The path is walked in faith when we allow Jesus to be Lord. We must align ourselves with the word of God, which is Jesus Christ, for he himself is the truth.

Jesus walked through hell to fulfill the promises of the Father to us. He walked through the rejection of men, and he walked through the rejection of the Father, when he became a curse for us. He took all of our sins, all of our fears and all of our shame upon himself. He did this alone, in humble obedience to the will of God. The pain he endured to pay the price for our salvation is unthinkable, and he endured it so he could save you and me.

We are no longer just talking about faith; we are now beginning to do the hard work walking in the faith and living it out, redeeming these areas of our souls, facing our fears which have kept us in bondage and unbelief for so many years. Do not listen to the spirit of fear, or the spirits of depression, and discouragement, for it does not matter where you are right now, it is only the direction you are headed that matters. You could be in the deepest pit on this planet but if you are going up, you are doing the right thing. You could be on the top of the mountains, but if you are going down, you are going in the wrong direction. It is not where you are located at the moment that matters; it is what direction you are traveling.

Most of us have not understood that real faith is the simple obedience to the written word of God, rather than obeying our fears, or submitting to our feelings which originate in the mind of our flesh. Our fears are toxic, they leave us helpless, they leave us overcome. They leave us full of doubt and unbelief, and they strip us of all power to operate in the kingdom.

We have more than David had when he faced the giants; we have the sword of the spirit, which is the word of God, and the anointing of the Holy Spirit, given unto us through the power of the resurrected Lord so that we may overcome these giants of fear, doubt and unbelief in our lives. We can uproot this darkness, the propaganda and lies that formed the belief system of dark counsel within our inner man.

Overcoming this system, which has left us defeated throughout much of our lives, is the central issue of the kingdom. Walking out our closest relationships in true love is his one new commandment to us. We were told in Scripture, if we do all things and have not love, we are nothing. If we prophesy and know all things and have not love, we have done nothing. Only that which was done through the Holy Spirit and through genuine love is of any lasting value in the kingdom. Everything else is wood, hay and stubble or worse. In the spiritual reality, the only truth is love, and everything else is of the lie.

THE BROKENNESS OF THE CROSS

We must determine to be intentionally loving, empathetic, and be willing to share our own brokenness, so that we might experience the brokenness of Jesus at the cross. For it is only after we experience the brokenness of the cross in our own lives, that we can truly experience the power of his resurrection working within us.

We look up to some of the greatest men in Scripture, to the men of God who have gone before us, and one of my favorites is Jeremiah. In the first chapter, we read that Jeremiah came forth out of the priesthood; he was a son of one of the priests in the land of Benjamin, and the word of the Lord came to Jeremiah in which God said: "before I formed you in the belly I knew you, and before you came forth out of the womb I sanctified you and I have ordained you a prophet to the nations."[61] Jeremiah was an awesome man of God, and the Lord spoke to Jeremiah and said "do not be afraid of them, for I am with you to deliver you."[62]

The Lord touched Jeremiah's mouth and said "I have put my words in your mouth, and I have set you this day over the nations and the kingdoms, to root out, and to pull down, and to destroy and to throw down, and to build and to plant."[63] The Lord came again to Jeremiah and said "what do you see" and Jeremiah answered God saying "I see the rod of an almond tree" and the Lord said unto Jeremiah, "you have seen well, for I am about to hasten my word to perform it."[64]

I WILL HASTEN MY WORD TO PERFORM IT

Once again, the Lord is about to hasten his word to perform it. Throughout the book of Jeremiah, we have the testimony of the Lord against the nations, for the Lord put his word in Jeremiah's mouth. But in the book of Lamentations, we have Jeremiah's word, and this is Jeremiah's testimony after his ministry as a prophet to the nation of Israel in which he says "I am the man that is seen affliction by the rod of his wrath."[65] In Hebrew the word used for *man* in this text is גבר, *gheber*[66] which means a valiant man, a warrior or a mighty one.

Jeremiah is saying "I am the valiant man who has seen affliction" and that word for *seen* means having experienced it. Jeremiah knew what it meant to be afflicted under the hand of God. "He has led me and brought me into darkness and not into the light." That word for *led* means to drive you and to carry you away; and the word for *darkness* means misery. "He has carried me into misery, sorrow, and destruction. Surely against me he turned his hand all the day, he made my flesh and my skin old, and he has broken all my bones. When I cry out he shuts out my prayer." This is Jeremiah, who was chosen by the Lord as a prophet over the nations, giving us his testimony after he completed his ministry. "He caused the arrows of his quiver to enter into my reins." And the word for *arrows* in this text is בֵּן, *bên*,[67] which means a son, or the people.

It was the people who had become the arrows that came against Jeremiah. The arrows which were shot into Jeremiah's loins came from the people that were around him, and they cut into his *reins*; and this means in his mind, his inner self. The arrows and the afflictions came into Jeremiah's heart and into the depths of his inner self.

Jeremiah exclaims "I was made into derision to all the people and their song all the day." And the word for *derision* means laughter, a scorned one, mocking, and to make sport of. Mocking Jeremiah was a sport in Israel. Jeremiah jokes were everywhere. Jeremiah was the laughing stock of the people all the day. The whole nation mocked him. They sang songs about him. They sang songs against the great prophet of God who they all despised.

GOD FILLED ME WITH BITTERNESS

Jeremiah testifies "God filled me with bitterness, and he made me drunk with wormwood. He broke my teeth, he covered me with ashes" and the word for *covered* means to humiliate; Jeremiah was humiliated, he was mocked, the people were like arrows in his back, and his soul was removed far from peace.

He went through this entire affliction, and then he had to witness the destruction of his nation and of Jerusalem. He saw the judgment poured out, his eyes running with tears, while his own life was spared, and then God revealed to Jeremiah all of his sin. He was a sinful man like all of us, a man born in the flesh; he had dark counsel in his carnal mind like the rest of us.

The Lord was revealing all of this to Jeremiah, and in the midst of the judgment Jeremiah says "remembering my affliction, and my misery, the wormwood and the gall." The word for *misery* means maltreatment. He was treated as an outcast by the people, and he says "my soul has them still in remembrance and is humbled within me."

REMEMBERING THE AFFLICTION AND THE GALL

All of that affliction and persecution, all of the misery and gall, worked its perfect work in Jeremiah, to bring him to total humility, and there his soul had them in remembrance. He remembered how he felt, as he walked through the furnace of affliction, which brought him to true humility. Knowledge puffs up, and if God fills you with all knowledge, you will become puffed up. Only love edifies, and only affliction brings true humility. The Scriptures declare that "if my people who are called by my name will humble themselves and pray, repent and seek my face and turn from their wicked ways, I will heal their land"[68] but the land is not getting healed.

Pride is the number one abomination listed in scripture. It is at the top of the list of things which God hates, and God removes it only through the furnace of affliction. Everything Jeremiah went through was for the purpose of humbling him. Those arrows of affliction, when the Lord smites us, when his arrow comes forth, and when it shoots forth, we get to decide whether to entertain the debate and we get to choose how we are going to respond to the affliction. Are we going to respond in our dark counsel? Are we going to complain? Are we to contend, and blame other people?

RECEIVE THE CORRECTION OF THE LORD

Or are we going to receive the correction of the Lord? Are we going to humble ourselves and repent, and turn from our wicked ways, or are we going to stay in the dark counsel of our mind? If we do, we will become withered, and dried up, and then we will be broken off like dead branches, and the women will come and gather them together and set them on fire.

The whole issue is our answer to one simple question: what are we going to choose to believe? Are we going to believe our own lying eyes, and our own false belief systems, or are we going to believe the word of God, and the truth of the Scriptures? This one issue is ultimately going to decide our destiny. "My people are destroyed for lack of knowledge" for they have become a people of no understanding, therefore the Lord rejects them and will not have mercy on them. These people are asleep, and they know not the time of the judgment of their Lord, and most of them, as naked virgins, are sleeping with no oil in their lamps.

Walking in the Holy Spirit is not debating doctrine; it is walking in the fruit of peace and love and the experiencing the fullness of the Holy Spirit. We are not going to get there through the power or the mind of the flesh. We have to crucify the flesh, and without the affliction in the flesh, we will stay in the deceptions of the carnal mind of man. The reason the Lord sends the affliction is he wants to save us from the deception of our own dark counsel.

If you look in the Scripture, the Lord lists the sins that are abominations before him, and the very first sin he mentions is pride. But pride is such a slippery little sin, it hides itself within, and it covers itself with religious robes of false humility. People are proud, and they do not even know they are proud. They can even be proud of how humble they are. Those religious demons will come in, and the proud in heart have lost the battle before they've even begun. I am just so impressed with brother so and so; he is such a humble man. Really? Try talking to him sometime. If you say anything he doesn't agree with, he is going to try to take your head off. That is not the sign of a humble man. But we can be so proud of our humility. These sins have so deceived us; we don't even know they are in us.

MY PEOPLE ARE IGNORANT IN WORD

The Lord spoke to me recently saying, "My people are ignorant in word, immature in their faith, and yet arrogant in their pride. My people are full of themselves, but I will empty them out." This is a nation of people, who are full of themselves, but they will soon be emptied out, and God empties us out through the fires of affliction.

And that is what the affliction is for, to pour us out. There is a whole lot of affliction, dead ahead for all of us, in the Great Tribulation. Many people are already experiencing the affliction of God in their lives, and many people are going through the fire, for God is purifying his house, and he is purging his people, for he wants a bride that is spotless and without blemish. So God is sending his fire, and he intends that we overcome in the process. The afflictions of the Lord take many forms, it could be sickness, it could be financial hardship, it could be through your health, it could be through false accusations, problems in relationships, it could be through everything. God has brought all of this in order to bring us out of our deception and into his truth.

The people that are totally deceived do not know that they are deceived. The people, who do not know the Lord, do not know that they don't know the Lord. The goats never once consider that they might not be sheep. They are so full of themselves, that they are totally convinced they are his sheep, yet the sheep are fearful, at one time or another, they fear they might be a goat. So if you have fear that you might be a goat, you are in good company, for every one of the sheep passes through that trial. But if you are convinced you are a sheep, and you have never feared being a goat, then you are probably not one of us, and you likely do not even belong among us.

So if you are one of the sheep that has feared that you might not be born again, and this is very troubling to your soul, yet you are seeking the Lord, praying daily, and diligently studying his Scripture, I have good news for you; that is the evidence you are one of his. So rejoice and continue to seek him with all of your heart for he is no doubt calling you. The goats never once considered that they might not be sheep, they are so full of themselves, of course they are sheep, even though they have no fear of God within them.

The dark counsel system can really twist us up in our own thinking, and we can do some really crazy stuff and be convinced that we are right in our own eyes. We can believe we did the righteous thing. There are levels to which the dark counsel operates within each of us, for this deception operates in all of us to varying degrees.

I want to address for a moment what happens when the dark counsel in the heart of man becomes so extreme that it begins to completely dominate the mind of a person. In this state, they fall under the control of religious spirits so that the lies inside begin to manifest in everything they do. If we should see any of this in ourselves, it is a call to serious repentance.

GIVEN OVER TO THE DARKNESS

The people who are completely given over to the darkness of this present age, and who are yet very religious, and some of them are the super religious among us. They are going to follow the beast in the dark days which lie ahead, thinking they are serving God. They will marvel after the beast, and they will worship the dragon who gave his power to the beast, and all the while, they will believe they are serving God.

In its extreme form, dark counsel manifests in what are called personality disorders, and more often than not, they are commonly found in religious behavior. _Behind the Mask, Personality Disorders in Religious Behavior_ by Dr. Wayne Oates is a seminal work on this subject. The following excerpts are very descriptive of how twisted the dark counsel of our carnal mind can become.

"These are ordinarily sane people, but they are wearing their sanity as a mask. They are religious people but their religion is a mask, it is not the outward expression of an inner possession, it's merely a semblance of sanity, it's a projection of Christianity but it is not authentic. Nor is theirs an authentic life. In the course of living, these people have developed ways of being, within the dark counsel of their minds that are not genuine."[69]

They are not real, for they are merely pretending. They are actors who are always on a stage. If they are supposed to act loving and kind at church; they will act loving and kind at church. But they also might display a strange facial expression, and body language that does not match the emotional message they are speaking.

The tension on their face or the pretense of their smile just does not seem to fit with their words coming out of their mouth when they say "we love you." It doesn't fit for a very good reason, they are just pretending. They hide the true feelings in their heart behind a mask which they use while they are acting. They have studied their part, and they have memorized all the right lines, but they are just pretending for they are mere actors on a stage.

There is nothing genuine about them; though their ways may appear to be human, their discomfiting expressions reveal the demonic shadows on their faces. The words they speak are colored with the voices of devils, for they can only speak forth lies, and they will never disclose the truth on the inside. In their hearts, they are against you, while they are blessing you to your face, in their hearts they are actually plotting against you.

A FACADE OF RELIGION

They are envious, judgmental, and critical while their minds are filled with nothing but negativity. They take what they can take, and they get what they can get. Theirs is only a veneer or a facade of religion, and in these hearts, the ritual of religion is more relevant than any real spirituality. The ritual is the most important part to them; it is all about the ritual, because for them, the ritual is all they have, for nothing else about them is real.

To their way of looking at things, God desires sacrifice more than love and mercy. In their twisted world view, it is all about acting religious. There is nothing about them that is true spiritually. They have no righteousness within their hearts. They have either wandered away from the straight and the narrow path, or they have never walked therein at all. They walk in a world of alienation, for they are lost in the dark counsel of their minds. They have been caught on the horns of death and despair which are the high places of hell, and their souls are trapped in the grasp of the devil, for they have fallen into his pit of idolatry and pride.

THEY ARE ALWAYS RIGHT

All the while, the dark counsel system in their mind, denies all of this, while they project their own evil onto everyone around them. These are religious zealots and they will judge you and condemn you if your doctrine doesn't line up with theirs. In their hearts, they are always right because they make the rules by which they live their lives.

These people can be quite likable, and they can be very friendly and obliging, but they are often quite deficient in terms of any real action. They almost never follow through on any of their great ideas, for they are really only good at one thing, talking. They talk a good talk, but when it comes down to doing the actual work of the kingdom, you will find that they want none of it. Their entire effort involves creating the right pretense, memorizing the right lines, and wearing the appropriate mask, fit for the right occasion.

ALL THE RIGHT WORDS

They are sometimes just too sweet, or too nice to be real. They have a manufactured personality which is always appropriate for the setting, yet all the while they continue as only actors on a stage. Many of them are very good actors, they know all of the right words to say and they can be full of great prophetic words, but they are also clouds without water, for they are the twice dead among us.

They are actually controlled by fear, and because they have been overcome by religious spirits, they tend to drift towards religious models or doctrines that could be described as based upon magical thinking. They are always waiting for their big miracle, but somehow it never comes. They are always looking for the magic word, for theirs is a magical view of the universe. Their poverty is not the result of their slothfulness, or foolish business decisions, but rather a demon yet to be cast out. There is no real substance to their spirituality; it's all façade, and religious veneer. Outwardly they are whitewashed sepulchers, while inwardly they are full of dead men's bones, and they spend their entire life looking for the right magic key to escape their dark reality.

These deeply troubled personalities are easily absorbed into the cults. They readily accept cult doctrines which are sold to them as secret mysteries, while their lies, which they have buried deep inside, make it impossible for them to actually discern the true from the false. There is nothing true about them, so they feel right at home with the lie. Some of them are found among the true church bringing their false doctrines and confusion among us. They argue you must pray in the Hebrew names of God, for that is their newest magic key to the kingdom. You must know the magic word, if you just find the magic key, or say the magic word, then the quest for the Holy Grail will be won, and then the power of the kingdom will be open to you.

THE SECRET NAME OF GOD

The knowledge of the secret name of God is the very essence of witchcraft. The witches in their pursuit of the arcane knowledge of the mystery schools sought the secret power of the occult through the secret name of God, because if they could find the secret name of God, then they could command the demons to do their bidding. The idea of using a secret name to wield the power of God is the essence of witchcraft, and has no relationship to the truth of the Lord in the kingdom of Light.

Today we have Christians who have come to believe they need to pray using the secret names of God and it is sad how easily some are deceived. You only need to humble yourself and pray, and you can do this in any language you want, provided you humble yourself and repent. It does not matter what language you are praying in; what matters is if you are seeking the Lord with your whole heart. But you must humble yourself and you must turn from your wicked ways, and you must repent, and you must believe on the Lord Jesus Christ. If you want to call on his name, using either Jesus Christ or Yeshua Ha Mashiach, both are fine, but do not go around telling other people they must pray only in the Hebrew name of the Lord. The Lord is the King of the universe and he has many names, even names that only he himself knows.

MAGICAL THINKING

These religious models of magical thinking are very appealing to people that have issues of dark counsel that are unresolved within them. The dark counsel created the conflicts within them, but they are so afraid to look into their own hearts, afraid of what they might find, they chose rather to look outside of themselves for the secrets to the magic kingdom.

Of course they are afraid, because of the wounds inside, and there is pain in facing the truth, but they turned away from the truth long ago, and they do not want to deal with the light. They are afraid to open the door, so instead they look for a magical way outside of themselves, to make the kingdom of God work for them, when in truth, they do not possess the kingdom of God at all.

THE KINGDOM OF TRUTH

There is no magic in the kingdom of God. The entire kingdom operates on one central principal, speaking the truth in love. You shall know the truth and the truth shall set you free. There are no magic words that are necessary. In fact the whole essence of magic is based on something that is hidden, something that cannot be seen, and this is the essence of the kingdom of shadows and it has nothing to do with the kingdom of God which comes within us through the truth in the light of day.

The kingdom of God is a kingdom of truth. It is about being honest, taking responsibility for your sin, searching your broken, sinful heart with the light of truth before the presence of Almighty God, then acknowledging and repenting of your sin and seeking to follow his commandments from a humble and honest heart.

SEARCH OUR HEARTS

If we ask the Lord to help us search our hearts, he will lead us on this inward journey. Then we will begin to see how truly wicked we all are, so much so, that every one of us could be called the least of the saints. In ourselves, we all belong at the bottom of the list, and there is not one of us that is above another. The whole lot of us are at the end of the line, and but for the grace and mercy of God, we too would be perishing. But God wants to heal us and deliver us from the darkness and sin within. The Lord wants to transform us, but first we have got to get real and then confess our sins, and we must repent and turn from them with an honest and humble heart. The truth confronts us, so we cannot hide any longer in our worn out religious dreams which is only a pretend religious system, and the only way out is to become brutally honest, and become a zealot for the truth.

TRADING THE TRUTH FOR THE LIE

The cross was brutal. Jesus was naked on the splintered wood and the nails pierced right to the bone. We have to come clean before the Lord and with each other, and we have to stop hiding anything. We have to bring it all forward into the light for pretending simply will not do. People who are lost in the dark counsel of their minds are afraid to go there, it is too scary, so they do not want any part of the truth, rather they make up a lie and that lie becomes their religion, but in reality, they are trading the truth for a lie.

The pretenders among us will manifest themselves as crowd pleasers, and some of them have learned to be star performers; you can see them on television, raising millions and millions of dollars. They are never offstage. They are the stars who must always be the center of attention, and who manipulate others for their approval. Through their subtleties, they maneuver like the serpent of old, they will manipulate, and exert pressure, to exact whatever they need and want from others.

There are many pastors that have fallen into this calling, and though they are nicely packaged people, theirs is only a cosmetic type leadership, for they do not care at all for the flock. They do not really tend to the sheep, rather they muddy the water, and shear the sheep, whether for their financial gain or the gratification of their egos, to feed their incessant self-worship. These pastors and preachers, who have no care or concern for the sheep, are politicians in the church, and salesman of the New Covenant but in truth they are only selling the new counterfeit.

These false hirelings can preach a good sermon, but their emotions are all pretend. You could know these people for years, and all the while you would be left wondering what is behind that mask?

THE CHILDREN OF THE LIE

These are hollow persons, for they are the children of the lie. They can act very lively and dramatic, and they often will exaggerate a great deal. Theirs is a grand prophetic vision, yet they are the only star upon their stage. Their grandiose vision often borders on the absurd. They are going to save Hollywood. They are going to take it for the Lord, but they are playing a baseball game with a ball of silly putty. Their ministries and their grand visions amount to nothing more than a circus act of spinning plates which in the end accomplishes little to nothing at all.

Their imaginary ministries have been confirmed by great prophetic words. Theirs is always a grand vision, but they easily become bored, so they typically abandon every calling before bringing about its birth, and then they are on to the next great vision. They love to talk about the great things they are doing or will do in the name of God, but in the end they do very little if anything at all.

They quickly form friendships, but once they become your friend they quickly become too demanding, egocentric or inconsiderate and inconsistent. They are drawn in numbers to the churches, for there they can find many religious forms for the expression of their dark counsel, and they will find many social support groups as well, who will support and enable them to continue under Satan's spell.

These people often have impaired memories, when you are out of their sight; you are out of their mind. They have moved on to their newest target, their newest experience, and their lack of faithfulness and loyalty extends to everyone to whom they have made a commitment, a covenant or a promise. If they borrow money from you, they will promise up and down to pay you back, but they probably never will. They would rather break friendship than have to face you. There is no covenant, or no promise, they cannot rescind at their will.

These are self-absorbed persons, they want little or nothing from others except what will gratify their appetite for adulation, or confirmation of their superiority. They call themselves by many titles, and oh they love their titles: Apostle, Prophet, Bishop, or Pastor, and they even have an Apostate Counsel of Deluded Elders, while the greatest men of God who have walked this earth were men who merely called themselves brother.

Not these packaged personalities, they love to add to their titles; they insist on their titles, and they are always grasping for more. They live a self-admiring and self-sufficient life; they draw a sense of security from perceiving themselves as above the crowd. They are disdainful and superior to others, for they are stronger, brighter, richer and certainly more important than others. These people are utterly lacking in any capacity for self-evaluation or empathy, and they will not and cannot accept any criticism. They are utterly unable to see themselves in any of the pages of this book.

They live lives of grandly assumed entitlement, whereas reciprocal covenants and genuine concern for other people or the rights of others are disregarded, while they demand special treatment for themselves. Any capacity for empathy is missing. Good men use the world to enjoy God; wicked men use God to enjoy the world. These people love things and use people to achieve their own happiness and pleasure, whereas healthy people love others, while using the things they have for the benefit of everyone.

To the person embroiled in the dark counsel of their mind, religion is magic and they have become the magician. They are intoxicated with the possibility, but they are terrified when confronted with the requirement of putting up or shutting up in regards to all their spiritual notions. They are dreamers, for they dream a lot, but they accomplish very little.

IMPARED CAPACITY FOR LOVE

They expect others to do the actual work to accomplish their dreams. They are infinite dreamers, who fail when confronted with the realities of life. They then turn to scapegoat others, to defend their honor, because when they fail, it is always someone else's fault. They will scapegoat anyone to protect their paper house of egotism. The bedrock for these wounded souls is a deeply impaired capacity for commitment and love of other people. The ordinary rules of human interaction are set aside by these self-absorbed persons. They are above the law. It is beneath their station in life.

A much more serious, but less easily detected version of this behavior is the authoritarian religious person's claim to infallibility as to both their own beliefs and doctrines. Theirs is extremism, and this will manifest in the form of "the Lord told me" and how do you question the Lord? Except the Lord did not tell them anything. They simply lied or perhaps they heard from one of their religious demons, or they spoke the word out of their own broken divided heart. They will take on extremism, and this extremism goes to the level of infallibility of their own beliefs.

They are right about everything. They do not even consider the possibility that they could be wrong, or that they have ever been wrong. Their identity is one of extremism and it demands the rejection of any criticism. Teach ability? Empathy? Towards anyone, who they perceive as weaker in their game of power, that is out the window. These people really do believe in Jesus Christ, but they view themselves as personally exempt from his demands. They are free to do as they please, pursuing their goals of self-gratification. They can lie, cheat, steal or whatever.

In their worldview, there is Jesus and them, then everyone else. And for some of them, it is not even in that order. They are free to do whatever they please, they can exploit you financially, they can exploit other people sexually, and they will exploit their position or anything else that belongs to anyone as long as it fulfills their desires or infallible claims.

THE INFALLIBLE ONES

Infallibility is theirs alone and they know it. These souls learned to live early in life with caregivers who could not be trusted, so they had to become a rugged survivalist. Their dark counsel was formed in a place of great deprivation, where they realized they had to force or manipulate others to get what they wanted, and they were never willing to take that to the cross. Intimidation is their tool of choice; verbal or physical, whenever their low frustration tolerance is slightly tested, and they are even given to vengeance. These people are calloused to social contracts and covenants to others; in their opinion, any contract or covenant is voidable at their discretion. They live for personal power and control over the whole of the social scene they survey.

GRACIOUS AND CHARMING

If acting gracious, cheerful and charming will maneuver and subjugate a person to their will, then that is the way to go. But if being cheerful, gracious and loving fails, frustration of their will for power will easily turn into furious, vindictive attacks. People are tools for their power. Religion is subordinated to the absolute necessity of a personal need to control, and their antisocial behavior flows into every area of their life. They will always resist authority. They will come in agreement with you, but in the end they will never submit to anyone. These are some of the extreme forms of the satanic belief systems which form in the dark counsel of the seriously maladjusted ones among us.

Now the person that is seriously sick will never recognize any of what you just read in them. The rest of us might recognize some of our sinful behavior in some of what you just read, because the self-absorbed carnal man will manifest some of those things from time to time. He pretends to be right, but is wrong, while he projects his sin onto to anyone who looks remotely similar. He is not open to correction, rather he hides his sin, and he runs from the light, lest the true nature of his deeds be discovered.

And when the Lord puts him in the fire to purge out all of these lies and bring him to true repentance, he never stops debating with it. He becomes angry, and he will not submit to the discipline of the Lord. He also will not repent of the secret sins within, and even affliction does not cause him to humble himself. He stands proud, and he does not break those religious systems like chalk stones. He does not burn down the false religious altars, and he does not tear down the high places erected in his heart. He is always looking for someone else to blame for the trouble in his life, and then he moves on down the road.

AS SERIOUS AS IT IS DEADLY

The dark counsel of fallen man is as serious as it is deadly. It is the sin nature in all of us, and it is more wicked than we can imagine. It is downright ugly. This dark counsel will also fool the unsuspecting; you could be in a relationship, with your children, spouse, or family members, and you can behave in ways you think are right. You could take the high ground, convinced that you are right, but time will pass and the Lord will open your eyes and let you see the whole picture, and you will realize you did not respond at all in love, and you did not respond at all in accordance with the character of Jesus. You were not walking in the spirit; rather you were acting out of your own fears or pride, lost in your own carnal nature, while you had the whole thing rationalized in your mind. You knew you were right for all the right reasons and you went ahead and said or did whatever you said or did, persuaded beyond measure you were doing exactly the right thing and when God finally opens your eyes, you are going to be blown away, at how far wrong you have been.

On that day you're going to weep, if you are anything like me. At first, you will begin to pull out your hair, and scream "No Lord, it's not true! It can't be true!" But then the Lord is going to say to you "It is true..." and then you will bow your head, and finally humble yourself, as he begins to show you there is more. If you're anything like me, you're going to weep, and then you are going to begin to finally die to the flesh, and become desperate in your search for the narrow way that leads to life, and you will be screaming for the power of the cross to set you free. And you will cry out like the Apostle Paul, "O wretched man that I am! Who shall deliver me from the body of this death?"[70]

THERE MUST BE SOME WHO ENTER IN

Maybe there are a few believers out there who are walking in total victory and they have already overcome all the dark counsel within. They have already done the hard work and they have conquered the land within their soul. The giants are already defeated, and that toxic mess that we call the belief system of the world is no longer affecting their lives. But I think they are the few. The Scripture declares, there must be some who enter in, so there are always some who are overcoming.

But the experience of the majority is that we are still in the battle. Herein lies all of the issues of our heart, for we are a group of wounded people, who have been stepping on each other, and re-wounding each other, and if we keep operating in the flesh, we will just keep re-wounding each other again and again. Bringing one offense after another as this is the hour when the many shall become offended, and we will find that our own actions are just one more part of the problem.

THEY THAT LOVE THY TRUTH

The Scripture says "Great peace have they which love thy truth and nothing shall offend them."[71] Even when Jesus was being persecuted, beaten, tortured, and ultimately crucified, the Lord was never offended. He never once lashed out, he never responded in the flesh, and he never once acted within the dark counsel of fallen men. He prayed for his persecutors, and asked his Father to forgive them, for they *did not know* what they were doing.

And *not knowing* is the whole essence of dark counsel, because we do not know what we are doing. We are operating in a mindset of deception, for the carnal mind is deceived. We see through a mirror dimly, motivated by the passions and desires of the beast nature. We do not see what is in our own hearts; we think we know, but we do not know. We think we understand, but we do not understand. You cannot even understand what is in your own heart, for it is deceitfully wicked, and who can know it.

TRUST IN THE LORD WITH ALL THY HEART

Unless you pray and diligently seek the help of the Lord to uncover what is in your heart, you can have a denial system so deep, you could call black, white and you could call the truth, a lie. This is why the Scripture says "Trust in the Lord with all thine heart; and lean not unto thine own understanding but in all your ways acknowledge me, and I will direct your path."[72]

We simply do not know; and that is the most amazing part of this revelation. We can operate in the Holy Spirit, and we can have revelation of truth from God. But as soon as we come out of the spirit and go back into our natural mind, we remain a victim in bondage to the dark counsel that yet remains there. And in those dark places, which have not yet been redeemed by the Lord, we can operate under total deception, and have no idea what we are doing, or how badly we are hurting the people around us.

We do not know what is in us, nor can we know the real motives of the people around us. The people that are walking in pretense and that are wearing a mask; the predators in the pulpits, and on television, the national ministry names, many of them are satanic. They were sent by Satan, and by the Illuminati; to deceive the church, and to steal all the money from the tithe, so that the wealth of the church would not go to true missions, but rather into buying 35,000 square foot homes, exotic animals, pornography collections, $5,000 pens, and collections of expensive jet airplanes.

DECEIVING AND BEING DECEIVED

The pastors who are using and abusing their flocks, and feeling entitled to do so; the Christians who are using and abusing other believers, and feel entitled to do so, all of us, when we are defending our pride and sitting high in our saddles, we simply are being deceived. Deceiving and being deceived.

"But evil men and seducers shall wax worse and worse, deceiving, and being deceived." [73]

We were told to be servants to one another and to love one another; yet all of us have been deceived to various degrees. I would assume most of my readers know enough to turn off most of the television evangelists because the majority of them are mass marketing the new counterfeit and they have nothing to do with the New Covenant. They are just part of this wicked system, and just another cog in the machine being built by the beast, or more precisely by the woman riding the beast, who has built her house in the land of Shinar, which is in the plains of

Babylon. There are a few speaking the truth, but the real ministers of the Lord are in the wilderness now, and the remnant will be led to find them soon.

A good litmus test for how well we are doing in dealing with our own dark counsel is this: if we are spending more time talking about the sin of other people then we are dealing with it in our self, we probably have not come out of the dark counsel. Our business is to get rid of the sin in us and the more you move towards true repentance and the more you humble yourself, the less the sin in the people around you will bother you. It will not be your focus and you will feel compassion and grace for people, and their sin will no longer offend you. He that is been forgiven much, will love much, and he that has been forgiven little, does not love at all. That is the testimony of this generation: this is the generation that has not been washed from their sins, and does not love at all, for in the time of the end, because wickedness abounds, the love of the many has grown cold.

THE VALLEY OF DECISION

There comes a time in everyone's life when they have to take responsibility and decide whether they want to continue on the path that has created all of the devastation and all the destruction, or take the path of life, and experience love and peace and joy from God. Ultimately, everyone comes to the valley of decision, where we have to choose. Some people find their way there sooner, others later, and some never come at all. How do we make a fresh start with all of that darkness still within? We have got to forgive and release all of the wounds and all of the resentments and all the anchors to the past.

We have to make a decision to take the risk and trust each other; even when it is scary, and even when we do not think we know how to do it. We still have to step out of the boat and begin to walk on the water, and know that Jesus is there. It may feel like your life is falling apart, but it is not falling apart, it is falling into place.

God is waiting for us to take that first step, to take a leap of faith and he will help us. And if we fall, he will catch us, but it is up to us, and we have to take the responsibility. We have to take the action, and it is not going to come from simply wanting it to happen. We have to decide what we are going to believe, and how we are going to live in the final days of our lives.

The Ministry of Death

The man that wandereth out of the way of
understanding shall remain in the
congregation of the dead.
Proverbs 21:16

The congregation of the dead has bibles in their church pews and they gather together on Sunday to hear a man preach out of his carnal mind, teachings which have come forth as fruit from the tree of the knowledge of good and evil. The apostate ones listen intently to the deceivers which have come among them, trusting in a salvation based upon the doctrines of devils, all the while believing they are following the Scriptures.

Their teachers are modern day Pharisees, who believe they have found salvation through their knowledge of the word of God, while their hearts have been hardened by the deceitfulness of sin, and the understanding of their minds has been blinded by the mind of the flesh within. Their ministry was appointed as the only portion given unto the people who are found within the congregations of the dead.

MULTITUDES IN THE VALLEY OF DECISION

Multitudes are lost in the valley of decision; they are the *many* who seek to enter the kingdom through the wide road which leads to destruction, for only a "few" are found seeking to enter through the narrow gate, and walking on the straight and narrow way. Some of these people believe they are spirit filled and call themselves Pentecostal or Charismatic, having convinced themselves they must be operating in a ministry of life, because they operate in supposed works of power. Even unto many of them, on that day the Lord is going to say "depart from me, you workers of iniquity, for I never knew you" They will be astonished to learn, that all along, they too had their part among the congregation of the dead.

The works which they did, which they thought were done by the hand of God, were actually works of darkness, performed within a counterfeit covenant, and the final fulfillment of the great falling away foretold in Scripture, which has manifested itself in the present day as the Ministry of Death. They will fight you to defend this ministry. They will attack you if you challenge the fundamental scriptural errors that are the underpinning of the paradigms of all of these deceptions. The Scripture truly declares, there is a congregation of the dead, and in our generation, it has literally become a mega-church.

There are entire churches given over wholly unto these deceptions, and they have Sunday services, and Sunday school for the kids, a vibrant community outreach, and they have all their programs. They sponsor their Halloween harvest nights for the children, thinking nothing of bringing pagan traditions within their sin friendly churches. Some of them claim to operate in the "spirit" and yet they too are among the congregations of the dead.

This is terrifying to the true believers, for there are multitudes of people professing to be born again Christians, who will perish for all of eternity, because all the while, their faith was in lies, and not in the one who is Himself the truth. They are children of the lie, who having never received the love of the truth, remained within the congregation of the dead.

The enemy of our souls resists any teaching which might uncover this truth, for this is one of his central deceptions and he is truly fearful that people might actually figure out the simple truth that you do not have to stay in the congregations of the dead. You can quit that church, and if you are attending a fellowship of the dead, you should find a new church.

THERE ARE TWO ROADS
FROM WHICH WE CHOOSE

There are two roads before each of us, and from among two paths we all must choose: the wide road which leads to destruction, where the many seek to enter in, and the narrow way which leads to life, where only a few there be who find this way. The people on the wide road are believers, but they do not know the Lord; they only know his name. These are the multitudes that have never been born again, and whatever version of Christianity they believed in, it did not include Jesus, nor did it include being born again by the Holy Spirit. In truth, all their faith gained them was a seat among the congregation of the dead.

Understanding of Scripture does take time and careful study; you cannot be casual about trying to understand the Lord and the deep things of God which are part of His covenants with his people. Much of the scripture was sealed up, and requires the Holy Spirit, and if you do not have His Spirit speaking to you through the word of God, you will be unable to hear the *Rhema* voice of the Lord when you open your bible. Without a personal relationship with the Lord, you will end up on the wide road that leads to destruction, and your life will end in one of the congregations of the dead.

LET US BEGIN WITH THE TRUTH

And if you appoint yourself a minister, and you go into the ministry without the anointing of the Holy Spirit breathing God's living word into your life, yours will be a Ministry of Death. There are people today that are pastors, or they call themselves bishops, prophets or apostles, and all they really have is a ministry of death because they are ministering in the flesh and the flesh profits nothing. The best we can achieve in the flesh is wood, hay and stubble and it will all be burned up on the Day of the Lord, for it is worthless. So let us begin with the truth, and then we will uncover the lies.

"In the beginning was the Word, and the Word was with God, and the Word was God. The same was in the beginning with God. All things were made by him; and without him was not anything made that was made. In him was life; and the life was the light of men. And the light shined in darkness; and the darkness comprehended it not." 74

In the beginning was the word, *Logos*, and the Logos was with God, *Theos*, and the *Logos* was *Theos*. Jesus Christ is the living word of God, and all things were made by Jesus Christ, for only in him is found the life. Jesus Christ is the life, and only through him comes the ministry of Life. Jesus is the way, the truth and the life, and no one may come to Father by any other way and every ministry that is not of him, and through him, is a ministry of death.

THE DARKNESS COMPREHENDED IT NOT

And His life is the only light of men, but the darkness comprehends it not. The darkness does not comprehend the light, for those who remain in the darkness, cannot understand the light of truth. The word in this text is *kat-al-am-ban'-o* and it means to possess, to understand or to comprehend and perceive.

The people who are found within the congregation of the dead, and particularly the leadership of the Church of the Dead, those who are in a full time ministry of death, as pastors and teachers, cannot comprehend the light of God's truth for they only walk within the darkness of their own minds, and not in the Spirit of God, and therefore they have no light within them.

The Lord referred to them as men whose eyes were evil, and thus their entire lives, and everything that they touch, and all that they do is only full of darkness. "The light of the body is the eye: therefore when thine eye is single, thy whole body also is full of light; but when thine eye is evil, thy body also is full of darkness."[75]

They minister only through the letter of the word, for they have not the Spirit of God in their lives, so they only minister out of the written word, as understood through the dark counsel of their mind, and not by the Spirit of Truth.

Paul described the ministry of the law, which was written in the stone tablets as a ministry of death, while the ministry of the New Covenant is a ministry of life, for it is by the Holy Spirit of God. The Lord "has made us ministers of the New Testament; not of the letter of the law, but of the spirit of God: for the letter kills, but only the spirit gives life. But if the ministration of death, written and engraved in stone, was glorious, so that the children of Israel could not steadfastly behold the face of Moses for the glory of his countenance; which glory was to be done away: How shall not the ministration of the spirit be more glorious?" [76]

The ministry of death is only of the darkness; therefore the only works which come forth from it are the works of darkness. Every seed bears fruit according to its own kind, thus the ministries which are from the darkness cannot bring life, and they can only bear fruit after their own kind. Thus they can only bring forth death, for the darkness does not ever comprehend the light.

BEARING WITNESS OF THE LIGHT

"There was a man sent from God, whose name was John. The same came for a witness, to bear witness of the Light."[77] God has sent his light of truth into this dark world, but we can only understand it when we come out of the darkness in our own hearts.

That is the purpose of this book, to bear witness of the light, and by the power of God's spirit, I shall bear witness of Him, for He alone is the light that has come into the world. "And as many as received him, he gave them power to become sons of God" and he gave them power to comprehend the light. The sons of God are not born by the will of the flesh, or by a decision of man, for as the Scripture declares they "were born, not of blood, nor of the will of the flesh, nor of the will of man, but of God."[78]

THE WILL OF MAN

A man may choose to become a Christian through the will of his mind, but he cannot be born again through the will of man. But we must be born again if we want to receive the true life of God. Any other conversion is a counterfeit, and there are many who believe, who have never been born again into a new life in him.

The *I will* statements in the minds of men are not going to get us past the deceptions of this world. You cannot be born again through the will of the flesh and you cannot do the works of the Kingdom through the will or the power of the flesh. Everything that comes from the flesh profits nothing including your will power. The kingdom of God does not come through the will of men, or through the will of the flesh, for the power of the flesh profits nothing. The ministry of death is nothing more than the ministry of men, who are pretending to do the works of God in the imagination of their minds.

GRACE AND TRUTH

The ministry of Jesus Christ is the only true ministry of God. His is a ministry of grace and truth which only comes through the power of the Holy Spirit. "And the Word was made flesh, and dwelt among us, and we beheld his glory, the glory as of the only begotten of the Father, full of grace and truth. John bare witness of him, and cried, saying, this was he of whom I spoke, He that comes after me is preferred before me: for he was before me. And of his fullness have all we received, and grace for grace. For the law was given by Moses, but grace and truth came by Jesus Christ."[79]

We received the law through Moses, but grace and truth came through the ministry of Jesus Christ. Herein is the dividing line between the ministries of death and the ministry of life. Every ministry and every bit of fruit, all of the words we speak and every deed that we do, every attitude in our hearts and even the meditations of our soul, is either from the flesh, or it is by the Spirit of Jesus Christ. The works which are from the Spirit of Jesus Christ, always come with the same nature as Jesus, and they always bear the fruit of His grace and truth.

ONLY THE SPIRIT GIVES LIFE

In 2nd Corinthians, Paul writes "The epistle of Christ ministered by us, written not with ink, but with the Spirit of the living God; not in tables of stone, but in fleshy tables of the heart. And such trust have we through Christ to God-ward: Not that we are sufficient of ourselves to think anything as of ourselves; but our sufficiency is of God; Who also hath made us able ministers of the new testament; not of the letter, but of the spirit: for the letter kills, but the spirit gives life."

The letter of the law only kills, for it separates us from the true life in God. The letter of the scripture without the Spirit of God brings only death. If you are ministering with your bible, through the power of the mind of the flesh, then you are in a ministry of death, and the letter you are teaching actually kills people. It is only the Spirit of God that gives life through the words of the bible; every other spirit brings only death, and the spirits of death love to minister with a bible in their hands. It is only when we minister in the Holy Spirit and are being led by the Holy Spirit that we are actually giving life.

The word in this text for *letter* is *gramma*, and it means a written word, a letter, learning, or doctrine. It is what we learn from reading the Scriptures with our carnal mind, enlightened with our knowledge of good and evil; it is the letter of the law, and the letter of the word when read devoid of the Spirit of God can only kill. It kills the reader, and it kills the hearer, because it is understood only through the carnal mind which is under the veil, blinded by the dark counsel of this ruined age. Only the Spirit can give life, and it is only when the word is filled with the *Rehma* breathed words of God that they go forth to bring life. This is the essential difference between the ministry of death and the ministry of life; the ministry of death is of the flesh, and the ministry of life is spirit breathed by the Holy Spirit of God.

THE FLESH IS UTTERLY CORRUPTED

For the letter of the word, the letter of the law, or the strict construction of God's word in the carnal mind of the flesh without the understanding by the Holy Spirit, can only produce death, because it is only understood through death. The flesh is completely corrupted and what does it produce? It produces religion! Look at the Pharisees, they are the perfect example. These men were professional Bible believers; it was their business, and yet theirs was a ministry of death. They thought they had the word of life, but they only had the word of condemnation in their hands. And the very word they trusted, in the end, condemned them.

Paul uses this phrase "if the ministration of death which was written and engraved in stones" to describe the Old Covenant Law, which is the Torah. The law itself was a ministry of death. Isn't that amazing! Think about this for a minute, how many people did the law save? Not one; the law did not save anyone. The law condemned everyone and then the law killed us. When the law came, death came, and guilt came, shame came and condemnation came, and then judgment came.

THE DEATH THAT IS IN US

Paul refers to the law of the Old Covenant, written in stone, as the ministry of death and yet the law was glorious. There is truth in the law. Paul was not saying the law was wrong, he was telling us what the law did to us, for it brought death to us. Not that there was death in the law – no, the law was perfect, righteous and true. The death was in us. If we take God's perfect law, and try to understand it through our carnal, sinful mind using the knowledge of good and evil which we received through the fall, do you know what you get: the religious history of man over the last six thousand years.

You get Cain killing Abel because his sacrifice was not accepted. You get one denomination hating another. You get division and contention, and you get people who only offer the sacrifices of strife and contention in the house of the Lord. You get fruitless lives, and you get trees twice dead, covered with only falling leaves. You get scores of false prophets, and you get religion without the righteousness of Christ. And this whole shooting match came right out of hell. That is why Paul called it a ministry of death, for the Old Covenant law, although righteous and true unto itself, produced nothing but death in us. Yet it was glorious, but this glory was to be done away with.

The ministry of the Law could only produce death in the people, which is why God provided a New Covenant, for the Old covenant alone could never have saved us. If Jesus did not come, and create a New Covenant in his blood, we would all be going to hell. The entire human race would be on the broad road of destruction and there would be no remnant saved. So the Lord had to replace the Old Covenant, although righteous unto itself, for it could never produce righteousness in fallen men, and that is the reason why the Lord provided a New Covenant, through the blood of Jesus Christ and the ministry of the Holy Spirit.

THE LAW DOES BOTH CONDEMN AND KILL YOU

Paul goes on to say "if the ministry of condemnation was glorious"; he is referring to the Old Covenant laws as a ministry of condemnation, and that was the power of the law, for not only does the law kill you, it also condemns you, and that unto to death. It is appropriate, for you do not kill people without a reason, and before the law kills you, it provides the reason for your condemnation, so the law in effect, does both. It condemns you, because you are unable to satisfy its holy requirements and then it kills you. And all of the sacrifices of all of the animals under the Old covenant were a testimony to the condemnation and the death which the law demanded of us.

When the perfect sacrifice came, when Jesus Christ laid his life down, he satisfied the eternal judgment of God. When Jesus died, condemnation and death was carried out in the infinite for when Jesus Christ died, God died. God took infinite condemnation upon himself, for when Jesus Christ, who is the eternal Son of God, and the infinitely righteous one, was condemned and died; infinite righteousness was condemned under the law, and infinite holiness and infinite glory was killed under the law on the cross of Jesus Christ as the penalty of our sin. An infinite price was paid for our salvation.

What was the value of the death of Jesus Christ? What value would you place on the life of the Lord? An infinite price was paid for our salvation. You cannot put a value on the life of the Lord Jesus Christ. His value is infinite, immeasurable. There is nothing to compare God to. What would you trade for God? There is nothing to trade.

AN INFINITE PRICE WAS PAID

An infinite price was paid to put to death not only our condemnation, but our death itself. The death that the law demanded of us, God killed it when Jesus died, and in him, our condemnation also died, if we would but enter in. We do not receive it automatically, we have to repent, and believe, and we have to enter in through the gate in order to receive it. We have to go through the door which is Jesus himself.

You cannot just claim the salvation of God which is the life of Jesus Christ in your life. You cannot just claim that you are born again, you actually have to be born again, and you have to do some things first in order to receive the salvation which is the life of Jesus Christ in your life. But with the ministry of death, there is nothing to enter into, and so there is nothing required of you, other than you just believe. It is just something you believe in your head, and in reality it becomes whatever you want to believe, for Satan has 31 flavors in his ice cream store.

Paul writes "the ministration of righteousness exceeds in glory."[80] The law under the Old covenant was righteous and true, but it did not minister any righteousness to the people. It was only when grace and truth came through Jesus Christ that righteousness and truth could finally be ministered to the people, and only then could men begin to be born again, not by the flesh, but by the spirit.

A SHADOW OF THE GLORY TO COME

The Old Covenant, which was written in stone, was a mere shadow of the glory of the New Covenant which is written in our hearts through the power of the Holy Spirit. Jesus Christ fulfilled the righteous requirements of the Old Covenant with his life, and with his death. Through Jesus Christ, God replaced the Old Covenant of condemnation and death, with a New Covenant of righteousness by faith, through which a new heart, born again by the spirit of God, could be filled with hope, love, grace, mercy, and truth.

This new life, into which we are born again, is born in humility, and birthed in the souls of the humble and broken hearted ones who having repented from their own dead works and have been born again unto God through Christ Jesus. The evidence of this new life is manifested in them by their putting to death the deeds of the flesh, learning to put on the nature of Jesus Christ, and learning to walk by the power of the Holy Spirit. In learning to walk in the spirit of God, we begin to enter into his very presence, and it is there he speaks to his chosen ones, and they hear his voice as he says to them, "I want you to stay with me."

THE KING OF RIGHTEOUSNESS

The faithful were never permitted to enter the Holy of Holies under the Old Covenant, but under the New Covenant, the Holy Spirit is placed within our spirit, as we are sealed unto God. In the book of Hebrews we are told that the Levitical priesthood was canceled by God and replaced with the priesthood of Melchisedec. *Melek* means King in Hebrew and *Zadok* means righteousness, so the new priesthood is according to the order of the King of Righteousness, and there is only one King of Righteousness.

The Old Covenant was replaced because all it did was condemn us, and that is precisely all we do as well, when we walk according to the mind of sin and death, which is the mind of the flesh. We only condemn each other. The enemy of our souls loves it, because in the flesh, all we have is a ministry of death, and who was it who came to bring death to us in the first place?

The Old Covenant has been done away with and has been replaced by the New Covenant according to the priesthood of the King of Righteousness. The King of Righteousness came among us to make a New Covenant that would not condemn his people. The New Covenant is so powerful that the Old Covenant was done away with; it was totally canceled, because it is now entirely useless, therefore, it was made of no further effect. It has disappeared. The Scriptures reveal the truth: the Old Covenant is now entirely useless.

So why would we want to go back to the Old Covenant when the New Covenant has been brought forth by the very Son of God through the power of the Holy spirit? Why are so many people confused by the false teachers who have come to tell us we have to go back to the bondage of the Old Covenant and begin to live again under the bondage of the flesh?

WE ALL MUST CHOOSE

God will not respond to the Old Covenant. In Hebrews we read that if we try to go back to the Old Covenant, we are at risk of losing our salvation. In the New Covenant, we have grace and truth on one side, while under the Old Covenant; we have condemnation and death on the other. Each of us gets to choose, but for me the choice is obvious.

The New Covenant of grace and truth has certain requirements, which are absolute. It requires that we repent and we are not supposed to obey our own will anymore. In the New Covenant we are supposed to stop doing what *I will;* that went right out the window for the born again believer. Jesus taught us to pray, "Our father who are in heaven, hallowed be thy name, thy will be done". What was the very first sin in heaven? Lucifer lifting himself up and declaring *I will.* So now we have a choice; we can choose God's will and learn to walk in the spirit under the New Covenant or we can choose from everything else which is some version of *I will.* In the end, all of the other choices are born out of the spirit of rebellion, where *I will* lift myself up and *I will* do all that is right in my eyes. All of the *I will's* originating from within the heart of man originate out of the pride of life, the lust of flesh, or the lust of the eyes. All of these things come from the *I will* side of life.

The life of the flesh is full of the things that *I want* or that *I will*. What stood between Jesus Christ and our salvation, after he had perfectly fulfilled the law of God under the Old Covenant, was the cross. He had to embrace the cross, the ultimate submission to thy will be done; submission and obedience to the will of the Father. This is the will of God, denying your own self-interest, making yourself a living sacrifice, submitting completely, enduring the suffering and through the obedience of the cross, learning to walk in righteousness in the meditation of our hearts.

SEPARATING THE TWO COVENANTS

What separates us from the covenant that could only condemn us, and then only kill us, is the cross. That is why God had to replace the Old Covenant, because he wanted to save his people. It was his will to save his people, and the Old Covenant could not accomplish that. That is why it had to go. It was only given to teach us righteousness and to show us our need for a Messiah, because in the flesh, God's righteousness and absolute holy standards, when codified in his perfect law, could only condemn and kill us.

So why is it that a large number of Christians want to go back to the Old Covenant in some form or fashion? Why are we all so tempted to try to walk out the New Covenant through the strength of our flesh, when the scripture tells us, our flesh profits nothing? Why is that? What makes some people think that you have to pray in Hebrew? What makes people think that we need to argue about how we keep the Old Covenant? Or that we should even worry about how we keep the laws in our flesh? There is one requirement of the New Covenant that is paramount: we must learn to do the will of the Father through the power of the Holy Spirit.

FORGET THE FORMER THINGS

If you want to go back to the Old Covenant and act like you are an Israelite believer three thousand years ago, that is between you and the Lord. If you are drawn to the Hebraic roots of the faith, and want to worship for ceremonial purposes as if you were a Jew, because you want to rejoice in the history and culture of the heritage of our faith, praise God! I love the history of Israel as much as you, but do not think for a minute that you are more holy because you dress up in ceremonial garments, for if you do, then you have fallen into serious error. If you are caught up in strivings about the law, you have fallen into heretical error and you are in danger of losing the New Covenant.

"Avoid foolish questions, and genealogies, and contentions, and strivings about the law; for they are unprofitable and vain."[81] The word for *contentions* is *er'-is* which means to quarrel, or to engage in vain wrangling: contention, debate, strife, and variance. The word for *striving* is *makh'-ay* which means a battle, an argument or a controversy, the act of fighting, strife, or striving.

AVOID FOOLISH QUESTIONS

Paul is admonishing us; avoid foolish questions and strivings about the law, questions of how we should keep the Sabbath, or how we should keep the feast days, for all of this is but vanity. The one requirement of the New Testament believer is to walk out the will of the Father through the power of the Holy Spirit, with a heart of humility filled with faith, hope and love, and everything else is sin. We do not want to go back to the works of the flesh. The Scriptures contain a number of apparent contradictions. In one place the word of God tells us to rest, to stop, to quiet yourself, and cease from your own labors while in another place the word says strive, knock, and ask. So which is it: am I supposed to strive or am I supposed to rest?

BE STILL AND KNOW THAT HE IS GOD

The Scriptures where God is telling us to cease and to stop, to be still and know that he is God, are speaking to us in the mind of the flesh. He is saying stop this non-sense, sit down and quiet yourself and learn to hear from my spirit, for only then will you be found walking in the New Covenant, which is the ministry of the Holy Spirit. Only through the power of the Holy Spirit can we get things done for the kingdom. Then you are free to strive in prayer in the Spirit, which the Scriptures call *travailing prayer* and your prayers will avail much, for you will be praying in the perfect will of God. Then you can go and do the works of the kingdom of God with the *Rehma* word of God on your lips. Then the word of the Lord will be found in your mouth, and your prayers can move mountains. When you lay your hands on the sick, they will recover, and when you cast out devils, they will actually leave.

STOP WALKING IN THE FLESH

Until we learn to stop walking under the power of the mind of the flesh, which has been completely corrupted through the defilement of our knowledge of good and evil, we will continue to do only the works of the flesh, because the carnal mind has been sold into bondage through its knowledge of good and evil. In the mind of the flesh, we only walk in the dark counsel of the fallen mind of man, and this darkness is actually part of our spiritual DNA. It came from the fall, and it is the original sin which is in the heart of every man, bringing only death within.

This is why the Lord said "if you want to follow me" you must walk through the power of the New Covenant. If you want to worship God, in spirit and in truth, you must worship him through the power of the Holy Spirit under the covering of the New Covenant, having been cleansed by the blood of Jesus, through the waters of repentance. Under the New Covenant, the

Lord Jesus Christ himself is the living manna that comes down from heaven, which is the bread of life provided to the elect of God on the communion table of the New Testament. It is there, that the Lord will pour out the living water of the Holy Spirit in our lives. And if you want that covenant, which by the way, is the only covenant left now as far as God is concerned, then you are coming through the New Covenant, or you are not coming at all. Under the New Covenant, you have to learn deny yourself, pick up your cross and begin to walk in the power of the Holy Spirit.

If you want to pretend that you are Jewish, or go join a congregation of the dead, and listen to some man preach a message that will tickle your ears, out of the ministry of death, then you can continue to walk under the power of the flesh, and you can go and do whatever seems right in your eyes. You can go anywhere you want, and do whatever you want in the mind of the flesh, but you will not be walking in the will of God.

WALK IN THE SPIRIT OF TRUTH

If you want to go back under the law, and back under a covenant of works, or righteousness based upon your works, then you are joining the congregation of the dead, and yours is a ministry of death. You can go anywhere you want in the mind of flesh and you can follow the imagination of your mind into all kinds of deceptions, becoming ensnared in the various traps of the enemy, and held captive in the many places of spiritual darkness upon the earth.

But if you want to walk with the Lord, in the grace and truth that is the ministry of Jesus Christ, then you going to have to do it under the terms provided in the New Covenant, for the New Covenant has superseded and replaced the old.

It is hard to develop the discipline to stop responding in the flesh and to wait for the leading of the Holy Spirit. The only people who can understand these words are the people who have received the Holy Spirit. If you have never received the Holy Spirit, try as you might to understand these words through the knowledge of the carnal mind, it will be is impossible for you.

If you do not have the Holy Spirit of Jesus Christ within you, then you cannot walk in the spirit of Jesus. You have to be in the spirit in order to walk in the spirit. This is why so many ministries look to the covenant of death for guidance and thereby become ministries of death. They do not have not the spirit of the Lord, and whatever ministry they do have, is a ministry of death because the flesh is absolutely useless.

DISCERNING THE DIFFERENCE

Those filled with the Holy Spirit can discern the difference between a ministry of the flesh and the ministries filled with the *Rehma* words of the Father. The ministries of death are like the Pharisees, where the people they minister to become twice the sons of hell. The people actually become gospel hardened, where the true word of the Lord can no longer reach them. The Scripture testifies "if any man has not the spirit of Christ, he is none of his."[82]

If you only know his name, and have not his Holy Spirit within you, then you are none of his, and when you read Scripture, and when you try to formulate your religious identity as a Christian, you will find your place on the wide road that leads to destruction. Everything you do on that road will be of the ministry of condemnation and of death, and you will not be able to comprehend or understand the difference.

Multitudes are perishing under this deception, for they all choose the wide road naturally. It is in the nature of man to do what seems right in his own eyes; this is how we respond in the mind of the flesh. There is no real fruit in the congregation of the dead, but there are plenty of programs.

THESE SIGNS WILL FOLLOW THOSE WHO BELIEVE

The Scripture declares these signs will follow the true believers: "In my name shall they cast out devils; they shall speak with new tongues; they shall take up serpents; and if they drink any deadly thing, it shall not hurt them; they shall lay hands on the sick, and they shall recover."[83] What do you find in today's churches? Do you find devils being cast out very often? You can struggle with demonic strongholds in today's charismatic churches, and if you go forward for prayer you may find a full blown witch waiting to lay hands on you. You can go forward for prayer and more often than not, it is prayer that changes almost nothing. There is one thing that all the Pentecostal and Charasmagic churches are full of today, a lot of hot air.

MANY FALSE PROPHETS SHALL COME

A lot of prophetic words are not of the Lord; rather they are heated from the fires down below. There is a lot of hot air coming right out of the vents from hell. Many false prophets were prophesied to come in this hour, and they have come. In many of the spirit filled churches, they no longer witness the gifts of healing or have the power to cast out of devils, but they are filled with the hot air of the false prophets blowing like the wind.

The ministry of the false prophet is the hallmark of the ministry of death. Many people think they operate with a word of knowledge, or a prophetic gift, and they are merely spewing out things from their own mind, from their carnal understanding, and it is not coming from the Lord at all. These people only have a ministry of death, and they are the killing people who listen to them. If you are a pastor, and you are not ministering to the sheep, rather you are ruling over the sheep, abusing them and fleecing them; you have a ministry of death. The word of God says "Woe to the shepherds of Israel that do feed themselves! Should not the shepherds feed the flocks? Ye eat the fat, and ye clothe you with the wool, ye kill them that are fed: but ye feed not the flock."[84]

These shepherds have a real ministry; they kill those who are fed of them. Theirs is only a ministry of death and they are spiritually killing people. "The diseased have ye not strengthened" for there is no grace and truth nor real help there. "Neither have ye healed that which was sick" for there is no healing in these ministries. "Neither have ye bound up that which was broken" for there is no deliverance or restoration of the wounded. "Neither have ye brought again that which was driven away, neither have ye sought that which was lost; but with force and with cruelty have ye ruled them." These shepherds had a ministry of death, masquerading as God's leaders. Woe unto you Pastor, who feeds himself and disregards the condition of the flock.

It is natural for men to read the Bible and perceive the entire revelation through the mind of the flesh. And what do you think comes out the other side? Nothing good! Pastors who feed themselves while they rule their people with cruelty, force and a body count: a lot of ministries keep track of how many commitments to Christ they get, but they never do the body count on how many lives they have ruined.

THERE IS A CONSPIRACY AMONG THE PROPHETS

"There is a conspiracy among the prophets in the midst thereof, like a roaring lion ravening the prey; they have devoured souls; they have taken the treasure and precious things; they have made her many widows in the midst thereof."[85] The false prophets have made many widows; many lives have been destroyed by their lies, and they shall all give an account soon.

"Moses put a veil over his face that the children of Israel could not steadfastly look to the end of that which is abolished: But their minds were blinded."[86]

The covenant of death and condemnation produces blindness. That is why the people could not receive the teaching of the Lord Jesus when he came. The religious leadership rejected him, for they were blinded. The religious who operate under the covenant of death reject the work of the spirit, for their minds are blinded. Even until this day, the same veil remains over everyone who walks under the covenant of death.

Countless people have been swept away by the various versions of this teaching that we have to figure out how to keep the law perfectly. People who have determined to work it all out in their minds, but the Scripture says we have to learn to walk by the spirit and not according to our own understanding. There is only one reason why these people will not come under the New Covenant; in order to walk in the spirit, you must first repent.

To operate in the covenant of death, you don't need to repent and you can do *your will* for the rest of your life. You don't have to say from your heart, *thy will*; rather you can have your will. You can have your own ministry too; you can even build a mega-church, and if you preach the right doctrines from the covenant of death, you can take in mega-bucks. Just tell the people they will get rich if they give you their money. You can have your own private jet and you can live your best life now, but the end thereof is death. You can do whatever seems right in your eyes, but in the end you will find, your eyes were blinded, and the end of that path is death.

A VEIL OVER THEIR MINDS

The ministry of death places a veil over your mind, and a veil over your heart. "Nevertheless when they shall turn to the Lord, the veil shall be taken away."[87] As we walk in the power of the Holy Spirit, the living word of God renews our minds and thus, we are changed from death to life. In the ministries of death, people are led by their own understanding, doing whatever they choose to do. And you can have whatever doctrines you want to believe. You can believe in a pre-tribulation rapture, or you can have a false anointing and scores of false prophets telling you that you are going to be rich. You can believe whatever you want to believe and do whatever seems right in your eyes, but it is all deception and brings only bondage. Only the New Covenant can set us free, and the New Covenant is by the Spirit of the Lord. "Now the Lord is that Spirit: and where the Spirit of the Lord is, there is liberty."[88]

This is the enemy's main objective: to keep you walking in the power of the flesh, and under the deception of your knowledge of good and evil. So many false prophets have come, and there are many people operating in the false prophetic. There is even a False Prophet list on the internet, and they claim to come in the name of Elijah and it is very popular with the people. There is a real prophetic ministry that is of the Lord, but the false prophets outnumber the real today, just like in the time of Elijah where there were 450 prophets of Ba'al for every true prophet of the Lord. The false prophetic words may have been well intentioned, but they are nevertheless, deadly. The false prophetic words have brought nothing but confusion and deception within the Charasmagic churches, where the majority of the people in these last days, have for the most part, gone insane.

JESUS SAID "I AM MEEK AND LOWLY"

Jesus said of himself, he was meek and lowly. The New Covenant is walked out in meekness and humility, whereas the carnal mind is puffed up in pride. If we are operating out of the spirit of pride, and giving out so called *prophetic words* which are not from the Lord, we are operating in the spirit of enemy and have fallen into the ministry of death. All of the sons of pride are animated by the father of lies, who is the devil. Oh, but they always seem so correct. Satan's lies are all so believable. He never uses ridiculous lies; rather his lies are always 98% true but 100% false.

The bait is nutritious for the fish, but what comes with it is the hook, and instead of getting a meal, it becomes the meal itself. If you operate in the ministry of the flesh, you are actually totally worthless for the purposes of the kingdom. Much of what we have all done in our lives, has been through the strength of the flesh, for our own benefit; and much of what the average Christian does is according to their own will, and for their own pleasure.

I have heard it all before: Christians have said to me I don't feel like praying with you. I don't feel like visiting the sick or feeding the poor. I don't feel led to fast and pray and I don't feel like picking up my cross either. I feel like pleasing myself. I will do that which pleases me, and when I am done with all my good pleasure, maybe I will have a little time for a bible study and maybe I will find a little time to pray. All the while, I will convince myself that I am following God's will for my life. I pursue my own pleasure but in God's name of course, and then I will claim that after all of this, I am still trusting in the Lord.

There are a lot of people that are going to stand on that day and say "Lord, Lord, we believed in you. We prophesied in your name. We even built a mega-church in your name. We had a sin friendly church where we were just like the world. We had the

Kansas City prophets come, and we had all the women who wanted to control the church, they all came and ministered at our church."

MANY WALK DOWN THE WIDE ROAD

These people did not know they were on the wide road that leads to destruction because they were walking in and ministering in the flesh. They believed they were doing God's will, and yet all the while He never knew them. They thought those prophetic words were from the Lord but Jesus will say to them, "I never knew you."

The Scripture testifies that many will say on that day "Lord, Lord, have we not prophesied in thy name?"[89] How can anyone prophesy by the Holy Spirit if Jesus never knew them? They cannot, for these are the false prophets, merely came in his name, and Jesus warned us, many would come in his name and deceive many.

In reality, the walk of the true saint of God is so contrary to the experience and the paradigm of the church in America that you could honestly say there is a night and day difference between them. The vast majority of the church in America does not walk in the Holy Spirit, they all walk in the flesh. The vast majority of all the activity that goes on in the name of God is of the flesh, and in the end, it profits nothing. The vast majority of all the so called prophetic words come from the flesh, or worse, they come through the flesh from Satan. The words of the false prophet sound good, good enough for you to think maybe it is from the Lord, and they are just wrong enough to deceive you, rob you blind and destroy your life.

Jesus Christ, under the New Covenant, has only commanded us to do a couple of things. The New Covenant is a lot simpler than the old. There are six hundred and thirteen laws under the Old

Covenant. How many laws do we have under the New Covenant?

A NEW COMMANDMENT I GIVE UNTO YOU

The Ten Commandments are still the outline of God's righteousness. They did not get repealed when the Old Covenant was repealed; they are still an outline of God's will for his people. So how many laws of obedience do we have under the New Covenant? The Lord gave us one new commandment. God has amended the Ten Commandments and now there are eleven. "Love one another as I have loved you."

One of the ways you can tell which ministries are in the flesh, for they all come in God's name of course, and they all sound pretty good, but one thing is really obvious if you just look carefully. Within our flesh, we cannot love each other as Jesus loved us. That cannot be done under the power of the flesh, for the ministries of the flesh bring only an offering of strife and contention in the house of the Lord.

What exactly is the Old Covenant? Is it the whole Old Testament? The word of God will last forever, so we are not talking about getting rid of the Old Testament Scriptures. The Old Covenant was given to men in the flesh, because the people did not have the Holy Spirit. There was a remnant anointed in the Old Testament times, such as the prophets, but the common person did not have the Holy Spirit; they were all walking in the mind of the flesh. The Old Testament contains the Torah, the books of wisdom, the historical text, which are admonitions to us so we do not make the same mistakes, and then the writings of the Prophets of God who prophesied even to the end of the age. So we are not talking about getting rid of the Bible. We are talking about getting rid of the mindset that we need to somehow go back and walk out the commandments contained in the Torah in the strength of our flesh. The prophetic writings, the books of wisdom, and the history of the nation are as relevant today as they ever were.

Part of the Torah was ceremonial, and part was sacrificial, which included the sacrifice system for the atonement for sin. Both the ceremonial laws and the sacrificial laws of the Torah have been cancelled. In addition, the entire Levitical priesthood has also been abolished. And the Ten Commandments written in stone have now been replaced with the perfect law of liberty written upon the hearts of men. No longer written upon tables of stone, the perfect law of liberty was also never to be understood through the mind of the flesh. For the mind of the flesh dwells in darkness, and it is entirely unable to comprehend the light.

The prophets of the Old Testament prophesied until the end of the age. The historical texts of the Old Testament, the books of Wisdom, the Psalms and Proverbs still teach us about the wisdom of the Lord. What has been abolished is the covenant whereby we walk out our relationship with the Lord subject to our righteousness being established by our works under the law. And the works of the law were all done through the strength of man, and according to the understanding of the carnal mind of the flesh.

What has been repealed is the mindset that we need to somehow figure out the secrets to keeping the commandments of the original covenant, as if that was the way to power. One false teacher tells all his followers that the reason they had no power in their lives is they have been praying in the English name for Jesus Christ and not in his Hebrew name *Yeshua*. That is the spirit and the teaching of the anti-Christ, because any spirit that opposes the name of Jesus Christ is of the spirit of anti-Christ.

The truth is, if you want to have power with the Lord, what you need to do is first repent, and then you need to forgive, because this is where the enemy is deceiving so many of us. Many of us are walking around with unforgiveness in our hearts, and the scripture is very clear, we are forgiven to the degree we forgive those who trespass against us. In the Greek, this means in like amount, in similar fashion, and in exactly the same measure. So if we forgive some of the people who have sinned against us, we will be forgiven some of the sins we have committed, and then you will be turned over to the tormentors until you are ready to forgive all of it.

FORGIVE ONE ANOTHER
AS I HAVE FORGIVEN YOU

This is one of the central requirements of the New Covenant: that we forgive each other. If you want to walk in the Spirit with the Lord, and with your body as his holy temple, you cannot also walk in pride. The Scriptures declare that the Lord knows the proud from far off. As soon as you stick your nose in the air in pride, the Holy Spirit is headed for the door.

So, does the New Covenant require that you learn to pray in Hebrew? Of course not! You can pray in Spanish, Chinese, French or whatever. How stupid are we? Do you really think God is giving us a vocabulary test? This is not a language class – this is a class on righteousness, and on mercy and love. God is testing our hearts to see whether we love the truth more than our sin.

All these false doctrines and false teachings flourish because people refuse to look at their own sin, and so they have no power with the Lord. Then they look for a magic bullet to fix everything. The real reason they have no power in the Lord is either because of unforgiveness, or because they have not yet turned from their sin. The key is true repentance, with fasting and prayer, and confessing your sins one to another. But people do not want to do that. So they gravitate to these false teachings, thinking that maybe if we strive over the Sabbath, or learn

Hebrew, then we would find the breakthrough we need. How absurd!

RAISING THE BAR

Under the New Covenant, the Lord did not cancel the Ten Commandments; he raised the standard for obedience. Instead of do not commit adultery, Jesus told us to no longer lust in our hearts. Instead of do not murder, now the Lord teaches us do not hate your neighbor. God did not cancel the law, he raised the bar. And he raised the bar so high, you cannot possibly comply unless you are walking in the Holy Spirit. And then he added a new commandment, love one another as I have loved you.

Oh, only that much? Do we love one another if we will not forgive each other? Do we love one another if we are slandering each other? No, we do not. Keeping the new commandment of love is impossible without the Holy Spirit.

Nor are we keeping the law of love under the New Covenant if we keep judging and condemning each other. But the people who are operating under the ministry of death, theirs is a ministry of condemnation, so what do you think they do? They condemn everybody. Their ministry is a ministry of condemnation where everybody else is wrong, and they alone are the righteous remnant. Theirs is the First Church of Condemnation, and they meet every Sunday and you will really love their cookies and donuts. No thanks, I will skip that meeting.

If we have unforgiveness in us, you will be able to tell, because the people or the events, where you were at one time wounded, will trigger these feelings time and again. And these areas will continue to bother you. It will fester in you and you will always remember it.

THE NEW COMMANDMENTS OF THE LORD

Let's go back to some of the new commandments of the Lord. First, love one another as I have loved you. That is no small requirement is it? How about the second new commandment, heal the sick. Good luck doing that one in the flesh. Not very many churches have a ministry of healing the sick. Now some people are sick because of the consequences of their behavior. God also sends sickness as part of the furnace of affliction, to turn us to righteousness. So, it is not always God's will for us to be healed. Job was afflicted and the Lord allowed it for a reason. But if there are no healings in a church, are they really walking with the Lord?

People take the Scriptures and simply assume it applies to them, but there are conditions to many of the promises in the word of God. The Scripture declares all of the remnant shall be healed, and people assume they must be part of the remnant. Okay, based upon what? Well *I want to be*. It is an *I want to be* covenant. I want to pretend, and call my pretense faith. Many people have pretend doctrines, where they pretend the word of God applies to them, without ever meeting the conditions for the promises of God laid out in the Scriptures.

THE WIDE ROAD TO DESTRUCTION

There are multitudes of believers on the wide road to destruction who call their pretense and their deceptions faith. But it is faith without obedience to the Lord, and a faith without the life of God's Spirit. It is also a faith without true repentance or holiness. This false faith also includes a life without the life of Jesus Christ.

I asked the Lord; what is the difference between those who are perishing on the wide road, and the true remnant who have received salvation? The Lord answered me saying, "These are they who have never received of my character, and they have never been changed by my words, and they have never learned to walk in my ways. I will say unto them, *lo ammi*, for they are not my people and I am not their God. These bring only an offering of strife and contention in my house." *Lo ammi* is Hebrew and it means *not mine*.

They are not his people for they live their lives for themselves. They spend all of their time and money seeking their own pleasure and following their own ways and if they give any place to the Lord in their lives it is last-place, and the only offerings they ever give him are from their leftovers. They walk in pride, for their knowledge of the Scripture has puffed them up, yet they have none of his love. They show none of his grace, and do not walk in his ways. They are the Pharisees of this last generation, and they are twice the sons of hell as their ancestors. They are the many who on that day will say "Lord, Lord" but the Lord will say unto them "I never knew you." All they have is a pretend faith where they pretend the salvation of God applies to them. They are the many who are on the wide road to destruction and all of them believe they are on the narrow way which leads to life.

These are people who profess Christianity. How many Christians do you know that will tell you "I know I am on the wide road to destruction. I'm a Christian but I really don't want to do the things the Lord commanded us to do. I want my will, so I'm going to follow Satan into eternal destruction, but I like the Christian version of going to hell, because it makes me feel better."

WE HAVE THE MIND OF CHRIST

All of the doctrinal errors, and there has been thousands of them, involve people taking a statement of Scripture that is a spiritual truth and assuming it applies to them when they have not met the requirements for the promise. For example, the Scriptures declare that "we have the mind of Christ" but this only applies if you are walking in the Holy Spirit. If you are walking in the dark counsel of the flesh, you have the mind of flesh. And if you are walking under the control of demons, you have the mind of the beast.

If you are walking in the Holy Spirit, then and only then do you have the mind of Christ. Does that mean you know everything? Does that mean you are always in the Holy Spirit? No. The Scripture says we have the mind of Christ, but the context of what was written assumes you are spirit filled believer who is presently in the spirit, and when you are in the Holy Spirit, you have the mind of Christ. When you are in the Holy Spirit, the mind of God and the word of the Lord will come forth from within your spirit as intuitive knowledge, and if you are very quiet within your own heart, you will hear the actual voice of God within your spirit.

LOST IN THE MIND OF THE FLESH

But if you are in the mind of the flesh, walking under the knowledge of good and evil, in the dark counsel of the fallen mind of man, you will only hear the dark counsel of this world, or the muttering peeping sounds of the spirits of darkness which are all around you. And in many cases, those dark spirits have open access to the compromised and apostate Christians of the last days.

Every word of the Lord will be confirmed by two or more witnesses, so that you know you have the truth. Many people run around declaring they have the mind of Christ completely devoid of the anointing, and they will also claim Scriptures simply by saying "I'm claiming Psalm 91." You do not get to claim Scriptures, where did that silly game come from?

IT IS REAL OR IT IS NOT

You either have the mind of Christ or you do not. You either are in the secret hiding place of the Most High God described in Psalm 91 or you are not. Claiming something different avails you nothing other than deception. It is real or it is not. I know a lot of believers who are waiting for promises which are nothing more than delusion. Pastors in Africa sitting at the end of a dirt road waiting for their Mercedes. They no longer visit their churches, now they sit and wait for their Mercedes. They have never driven a car in their life, yet they abandon their flocks, and they sit waiting for a Mercedes which will never come.

You cannot just claim that you live with God. The Scripture declares in Psalm 91 he who dwells in the secret hiding place of the Lord will abide in the shadow of the Almighty. You cannot just claim that you dwell in the house of the Lord. You either dwell with the Lord or you do not, and what you claim in regards to this matter is meaningless.

CONFUSING PRETENSE WITH FAITH

There are multitudes of believers claiming things which simply do not exist, and they have been taught that their deceptions are faith. And in a sense, it is true. Their faith is their deception, and their deceptions have become their faith. They have believed in the lie, and now they have come under the spell of the ministry of death. They are walking with the multitude on the wide road that leads to destruction. Their relationship with the Lord is one of head knowledge only, and they walk in a faith that is nothing more than pretense and pretend. Woe unto them, for the eternal darkness is reserved for them and all who follow after them.

You can ask them, where do you live? "Oh I dwell with the Almighty." Do you really? We will find out who dwells in the secret hiding place of the Lord in the near future when the severe judgment begins to fall on our country. If you really dwell with God, then you are going to be fine. But multitudes will find out their faith was based on fantasy. They have been lying to themselves and everyone else and it will cost them the total ruin of their lives.

THE LOVE OF MANY HAS GROWN COLD

The love of many has grown cold and sin has abounded, and people are bound by roots of bitterness, having been injured and wounded by the enemy, and they are walking with broken hearts. They have not taken these issues to the cross, and they have not received forgiveness in their lives and in the hearts of the unforgiven, the spirit of rejection and resentment is now in control within them. You are going to be rejected by many in this hour, especially if you come with the true word of God. The many are going to hate you, because your life and your words contradict the darkness within them.

One of the major stumbling blocks in this hour is unforgiveness. Because we have not yet confessed our sins one to another, these issues of unforgiveness and bitterness remain lodged within. We deceive ourselves for our hearts are deceptively wicked, we deceive ourselves and then we go fashion fig leaves of religious works, and we create these doctrines in our own mind.

Let us go back to the commandments of the New Covenant: the one new commandment was for us to love one another as he loved us. That is beyond our flesh. We cannot do this in the mind of the flesh. We have no more chance of fulfilling the law of love in the power of our flesh then we had in fulfilling the requirements of the Old Covenant in the strength of our flesh. We must be walking in the fullness of the Holy Spirit if his love is to be resident within us. And this is the sign of the true believer; they are walking in the spirit and the love of God. They are not angered, they are not bitter, they are not walking in unforgiveness for they that love his word, and nothing shall offend them. Under the New Covenant we have something more than a commandment given to us; we have power through the Holy Spirit. But we can only receive the Holy Spirit when we are born again and we can only be born again when we are ready to be dead to our life in the flesh.

THE DIVISION OF ETERNITY

Standing between the two covenants as the point in time which divides the two eternities, eternity past from eternity future, is the cross of Jesus Christ. This is the marker in time, which forever divides eternity. The point where the nails pierced the Lord and cut into the wood; that is the point where God pierced eternity. We went from a conditional covenant based on our obedience to a covenant based upon us dying to our self in him.

The cross of Jesus Christ is the place where God did business with our sin; and it is also the place where we do business with God. Jesus said if you want to come after me, and be part of my New Covenant, you will pick up your cross and follow me and deny yourself.

That message is not as popular as the lie that God really meant you could be rich, or that you could have your best life now, and all you have to do is give your money to the mega ministers who are selling a counterfeit gospel to a people who are perishing. Satan is really smart, do not underestimate him. He weaves his lies, the doctrines of demons, and they are cleverly woven, for the false doctrines and the false prophetic words are 98% true but 100% false.

What is the third commandment of the New Covenant? Cast out devils and overturn the kingdom of Satan. And what is the fourth commandment? Make disciples of men, people who have learned to walk in his ways. People who have been changed by his words and people who have received his character, his life, his love, his humility and his meekness within their hearts.

And what does the modern church do? Are the sick being healed? Are the people being delivered from their demons? No, those things are rare within the churches of these last days, so what on earth is happening here? The truth is for the most part, the churches in America are a mixed multitude where the sheep are starving for the true word of God, and where the apostates are comforted by the lies. And the people, most of them can no longer endure sound doctrine, rather they have turned to fables, and they prefer to listen to the pillow prophets spin forth their web of lies.

THE UNCLEAN SPIRIT AND THE PROPHETS

I am so tired of the false prophets, and I am so thankful the Lord is about to shut them up, for he is about to remove the lying spirit from the land. "And it shall come to pass in that day, saith the LORD of hosts, *that* I will cut off the names of the idols out of the land, and they shall no more be remembered: and also I will cause the prophets and the unclean spirit to pass out of the land."[90]

Zechariah speaks about the last days, which is our time, saying the Lord is going to remove all of the unclean spirits and all of the prophets out of the land in one day! Now, why would God take all of the prophets out of the land on the same day he removes all of the unclean spirits? We can understand why God removes all of the unclean spirits out of the land, but why would the Lord also remove all of the prophets out of land at the same time? Is that a coincidence?

Is this not obvious? In the vast majority of cases, they are one and the same. The majority of the prophets in this hour are all speaking from an unclean spirit of divination or they are speaking out of their pride; for them, it is a one-up-man-ship game. They lift themselves up over the people, and then they think you will need them. Most prophets are false prophets. And that has never been truer than in this hour.

TRUE WITNESSES ARE COMING

Jesus himself said in the last days many false prophets would come. There are many people within the churches running around and the only thing they do is prophesy to other people, stay clear of them. There are true prophets coming at the time of the end. These are the two witnesses and they are true prophets of God. I am not saying there are no true prophets, but the vast majority of the people who claim to operate in the prophetic are in fact false. This is precisely what Jesus warned us of when he said "many false prophets would come." False prophets ministering in the mind of the flesh, and in truth, all they have is a ministry of death. If you stay in their presence long enough, you will find their false words will kill you too.

The final revelation for most Christians in America will be the realization that what they thought was faith in Jesus, was really faith in themselves and in their knowledge of the Bible while they rejected the will of God and continued to walk in the *I will* of Satan. The origin of sin began when Satan said in his own mind, *I will* lift myself up in heaven. The essence of the new life within a born again child of God is submission to *thy will*. It is through the cross that the *I will* of the flesh dies. In the mind of the flesh, we want to rule over our lives, and over each other, and we do all of this in the name of God, of course. We rationalize all of this, hiding our sin under our denial. I am not abusing the sheep; I am just defending the pastoral authority of my ministry.

HOW DO WE GET FREE

So let us go back to the question of how we get out of the mindset which is operating in the flesh. How do we get free of this stuff? We are all dealing with this, to lesser or greater degrees, but all of us are called to overcome the flesh, the world and the devil, and these three are in reality all one in the same, for they all work together against you. In order to overcome the devil, and the world, we must first learn to overcome our own flesh nature. The ones, who have suffered and died to the flesh, have come out of these deceptions even as Jesus Christ learned obedience through the things he suffered in the flesh.

One of the ways we overcome the tyranny of the flesh is through prayer and fasting, in which we literally deny the flesh its source of strength and power. Left unchecked, the flesh naturally becomes religious and it manifests itself in the ministry of death, which is no good for anyone. The religious nature of the flesh is responsible for all of the Christians who are going to hell.

THE DECEPTIONS WITHIN EACH OF US

So how do we begin to come out of these deceptions that have ruined so many who call themselves by his name? How do we get past the deceptions within us? First, we must consciously recognize the truth about how deceitfully wicked the heart of man truly is. When we finally comprehend the extent of the darkness within our own hearts, then we will no longer trust in our own understanding, and we will begin to seriously seek the Lord for his help, for without the help of the Lord, we cannot escape these deceptions.

One of the ways God helps us is through suffering. The Lord sends affliction in our life. He told us "I chose you in a furnace of affliction", and part of the purpose of the furnace of affliction is to get us to the point where we are ready to desire the work of the cross. As long as we are walking on easy street, and our version of Christianity is just a love boat cruise, where every morning we break the fast with pancakes and whipped cream, we are not going anywhere spiritually. Without suffering and without the power of the cross in our lives, there is really nothing we can do, other than continuing to walk in the flesh.

The end of all flesh has come, and unless we find a new life in the spirit, it will bring the end of us as well. So part of God working his salvation in our lives is that God appoints us suffering to the point where we get sick and tired of the flesh. The suffering we experience in this life is directly related to the reaping of the sins of the flesh that we have committed, but God uses the suffering to teach us to turn away from the selfish, proud and arrogant way of the flesh. God demands that we learn to overcome our sin, and not just the outer sins, which are obvious, but we must overcome the sin which sent the Pharisees to hell, the inner sins hidden deep within the heart of man; the sins of pride, the lust of the eyes, and pride of this life, and those sins are almost impossible for us to find, because we turn our eyes from them, and we simply cannot see them inside.

THE REAL VICTORY OVER SIN

How do we get the real victory? How do we put to death the sins of the flesh? Fallen humanity is intrinsically in love with themselves. The fallen man, in his inflated ego and pride, is fully in love with himself. We think we are so special and we are inherently proud. It is part of the fall which has corrupted our carnal brain through the knowledge of good and evil, which then judges everyone else as wrong and where we alone are right.

How many people have you met who think they are always right? Have you ever met a person who thinks they are the one person on this planet who is wrong? It is not going to happen. Everybody is right, and they are all good people too! Right, a bunch of good people, who know everything, are all headed to hell for eternity. Something is seriously wrong with this picture.

The reality is we are not right, we are all wrong. We are wrong every day, and we are wrong in virtually every way, and we have all committed more wrongs and more sins than we are even aware of. It is our "stinking thinking" and our self-centered attitudes that cause us to literally wound the people around us and be oblivious to it as we pursue our own pleasures. It is the pride of life and God says it is the number one sin and an abomination before him. It was pride that was found in Lucifer that caused him to fall. This entire rebellion in all of creation came through pride; the fall of creation came because of pride.

LIFTING THEMSELVES UP IN THEIR OWN EYES

What do you think is leading these people to speak false prophetic words and bear false witness in the name of the Lord? Pride. They want to be significant in God's house, or they want the power and the glory. It is all about lifting themselves up in the pride of their own mind. Next, you have the lust of the eyes. I like your Mercedes, and I think I'll take it from you. That Learjet is even better. This stuff is attractive to us. After the lust of the eyes, next is the lust of the flesh. The lust for food, we worship it. The flesh is by definition a glutton, for the carnal fallen mind of the flesh is a beast; it has the nature of a beast. The Scripture calls it a "bruit."

EVERY MAN IS BRUITISH IN HIS KNOWLEDGE

"Every man is brutish in his knowledge."[91] Every man is *bruitish* in his knowledge of good and evil. The word for *brutish* comes from בָּעַר, *ba'ar* and it means consumed, or to be like cattle, or a beast, stupid and foolish. If the mind of the flesh is not put to death, in the end, it will consume you, and turn you into a beast. This is what is happening to our nation, and to all of humanity; they are being turned over to the mind of the flesh, and it is consuming the soul within them, and turning all of them into a beast, or a dog, which is a type of a beast. Dogs are friendly though, unless you touch their food bowl.

"For the pastors are become brutish, and have not sought the Lord: therefore they shall not prosper, and all their flocks shall be scattered. Behold, the noise of the bruit is come, and a great commotion out of the North Country, to make the cities of Judah desolate, and a den of dragons."[92] The Scriptures reveal at the time of the end, the pastors will have become bruits, and the flocks will have been scattered, and the cities will become dens of dragons, which is a picture of the demonic possession of the nation.

A COMMOTION IN THE LAND

The word for *commotion* is רעש, *ra'ash* which means an uproar of confusion, fierceness, and a commotion. This is a picture of people out of control, mobs of men with the mind of the beast, and indeed a great commotion is coming soon, upon the land of the beast. The mind of the flesh is the mind of a beast, and in many ways it is like a dog. It is a human version of a dog. It is a very smart dog. It is a dog that can talk. But it is a dog nevertheless, and it is always going to return to its own vomit. That is the best picture of the mind of the flesh, a dog. The old covenant was a set of rules for people who had the nature of a dog. Do not bite the other dogs and don't covet their bones.

When I am walking in the spirit you do not need to tell me, do not kill my brother. The rules of the law are for the criminals, and when we are in the mind of the flesh we are in the criminal mind. The word for criminal and carnal are very close in the language for a reason. They both come from the nature of a dog, which is the beast nature. There is no way that your beast nature, which is your fallen flesh nature, with its prideful mind puffed up with its knowledge of good and evil, is going to suddenly turn righteous. There is no way. It is not going to happen, not now, not ever.

THE MIND OF THE FLESH

The mind of the flesh will never become righteous, the best it can do is to become religious, then lift itself up in pride, or condemn a neighbor. They do not keep the Sabbath the way we do, so we judge and condemn them. In the end, the people who stay in the flesh, who are never born again, and never learn to walk in the Spirit of God, are all going to die because no one was ever saved by the law, nor will you be saved by walking in the flesh.

The Scripture says only those who are being led by the Spirit of God are the sons of God; if you have not the Spirit of God, then you are none of his. So if you have not walked in the spirit of God then perhaps you are not even saved. This is the testimony of the Scriptures. And this is the destiny of the multitudes who are perishing and who only know his name.

ONLY AS SICK AS OUR SECRETS

Let us talk about forgiveness, and precisely how do we give and receive forgiveness. You are only as sick as your secrets. Satan only has power over you in the areas of your life where you have not yet repented and confessed your sins one to another as the Lord commanded.

The Scripture says confess your sins one to another and it means exactly that. It does not mean tell ten people. God meant what he said exactly. If you have sin which you have never confessed to anyone, it is sin you will not yet conquer. Part of the reason is this, if you have deep-seated sin in your life, and you do not confess it to anyone, what you are doing in reality is hiding it. You are hiding it in your tent like Aiken hid the wedge of silver. You can confess it to the Lord, and that is good, but the Lord commands you to confess it to at least one other person.

In the church today, what percent of Christians feel safe enough to confess their sins one to another? Practically no one. And why is that? Because church is a dangerous place and most are afraid of being judged, slandered, having their character annihilated and being rejected. And why is that? Because so many Christians, who are walking in their carnal mind, have judged them, slandered them, defrauded and then abandoned them. And how many times has this happened? Over and over again.

That is why Satan is so invested in this issue of slander. When Christians slander each other and judge each other, he can create enough division and anarchy within the church that people will be afraid to confess their sins one to another, then he can keep the entire church in bondage.

People will simply walk in pretense in church, and they will be unwilling to confess their sins one to another, and then basically they will remain bound in their sins. The second way the enemy binds everybody up, and keeps them snared in the chains of deception, is to get them to hold onto unforgiveness. The process works, for the first nail the enemy drives into your heart is rejection or wounding of some type. Now, the Lord says immediately forgive so the sin does not stick to you. It is not even your sin, you are just the victim, but if you respond with resentment and unforgiveness, now you are adopting that sin, you are letting that wound literally bring the sin within you, and within your life. So we go from a wound to resentment, and if the resentment begins to fester, and if you do not repent and pull that out of your heart, it will begin to harden your heart and it will turn into rebellion and roots of bitterness.

UNFORGIVENESS TURNS INTO REBELLION

Why do wounds and rejections turn into rebellion? Because God commanded you to forgive, and if you disobey this commandment, you are entering into rebellion and you are hardening your heart to the word of God. You are in rebellion to the express commandment of the Lord under the New Covenant. At that point, Satan will come along and say "Hey forget about that, what you need to really worry about is how you keep the Sabbath and all the religious rituals. Why don't we go back to the Old Covenant?" He comes alongside of you, puts his arm on your shoulder, and says to you "I know you're having a little problem with the New Covenant, so I have a better deal for you. Let's go back to the Old Covenant instead. Look, it's a whole lot easier, and besides, you get to be right in your own eyes all of the time. What's not to love about that?"

He sells us a remodeled version of the Old Covenant, it has several thousand years on it, but he refurbishes it, and he tries to sell us a new and improved version of the Old Covenant, in which we do not have to forgive each other, and we do not have to love each other either. You also do not have the mind of Christ; rather you walk in the dark counsel of the mind of your flesh. But you are going to love his deception, because you get to always be right. And you know your neighbor is always wrong. And you never have to forgive him either. You can keep your pride, and you can still enjoy the lust of your eyes, and you can partake of whatever sin or compromise you choose, because Jesus will always forgive you, so you can never lose.

A COUNTERFEIT COVENANT

People are signing up for this by the millions, for in the counterfeit covenant, it is always you who is special. But this counterfeit religious worship will also keep you divided from God and his love. It is a knockoff version of the New Covenant, and yours can come with the special Hebrew only praying tapes. And you will really have the power of God if you learn to listen to the Old Covenant backwards. And people believe these lies. In the mind of the flesh we can believe anything we want, lost in a hallway of mirrors, and deceived in the imagination of our own mind.

This is what the enemy is doing, he is keeping people divided, and has made the modern church into a place where people are afraid to be open and honest and to tell the truth. The enemy wants to sever as many relationships as possible, so you feel alone and isolated, and so there is no one you can talk to. People within the church greet one another and they ask - how are you? All of us have the same answer, "I'm fine." Really? Is everyone really fine? Families are being destroyed, lives are being ruined, multitudes are walking under deception and running down the road to ruin and yet everybody says they are fine.

No, we are not fine. But we do not trust each other enough to be real, and we do not feel safe enough to tell the truth to each other, so, we all go to church with pretense. Many of us have left church a long time ago for all of these reasons. I used to pray, "Lord, they are your people. Keep them if you want; but please keep them away from me."

In the end, we all isolate ourselves, and in the place of isolation, we lose the ability to enter into the prayer of agreement and to confess our sins one to another. You do not dare tell anyone in church the real things that you are struggling with because you do not want to be wounded again, and you do not want to be betrayed, and you do not want to be condemned again.

You need to find a church or find someone who is a real Christian, where you can take the risk of obeying the Lord and confessing your sins one to another, and then go after this process of rejection and wounding leading to resentment and rebellion so these things won't harden inside of you, because if they do, they will grow into roots of bitterness.

You have to pull this out of your life, and spiritually take an axe to these roots of bitterness, and we do so by speaking to them and commanding them to be cut out of our lives, and then fearlessly facing the truth within our own hearts while being brutally honest with the people in our lives speaking the truth in love.

I WANT YOU TO TELL THEM THE TRUTH

The Lord spoke to me recently and told me "I am going to send you to my people, and I want you to tell them the truth." I responded, "Well that is kind of large. What exactly do you want me to tell them?" "I want you to tell them everything I said, and I want you to tell them everything I did. And then I want you to tell them everything you said, and everything you did as well."

God requires us to tell the truth and he requires us to speak the truth in love. He also requires that we no longer hide our sin within. These are the requirements if we are to walk in the Holy Spirit, and if we are not walking in the Holy Spirit, then what spirit are we walking in?

If we stop being led by the Spirit of God and go back to being led by the mind of the flesh, we will become animated by the spirit of pride. In the spirit of pride, I can tell you who you are speaking for, and I know he is religious; Satan is very religious, but there is no life in his religion at all. He is the Bishop and the chief Apostle over the congregation of the dead. He trains up all the pastors, and he sends out all the false prophets who minister within the congregation of the dead.

I WILL

The point is this, when you are ready to let go of the *I will* in your life, then you will begin to recognize that all of Satan's lies are just nonsense. The reason we do not have the power and the anointing flowing freely through our lives is because we are not consecrated. Part of our life is still invested in in the flesh because we are stuck in the mindset of the flesh, and ensnared in the wilderness of sin because of our pride and unbelief or unforgiveness within. When you are finally sick and tired of being sick and tired, and you are finally ready to let go, then maybe you are ready to get serious with the Lord and start actually fasting and praying about it, because this kind only goes out through fasting and prayer.

FASTING AND PRAYING

I fasted and prayed over four years consistently, on a regular basis. I do not know how many times. Sometimes I would fail. I would set out to fast and pray, and I would make it only a few days. Sometimes I would fail on the first day. I just could not do it, but sometimes I would fast and pray for a lot longer. I failed a lot, but I also fasted and prayed a lot, because I kept trying. At first it can seem like beating your head against a brick wall but gradually your head gets harder and the bricks start to crumble. Finally, you reach the breakthrough point where your heart begins to change, and you really do begin to forgive others because you do not want that bitterness in your life anymore.

The people we hold things against, they are not giving it a second thought. They have gone on with their lives and here we are holding their offense against them and holding the same sin over ourselves and it is contaminating everything and keeping us in bondage. The reason we do not get the breakthrough is that we are still harboring unforgiveness. God is waiting to forgive you, and God can wait you out. God is fine today; it is us who are suffering. The Lord does not enjoy the suffering of his people, but he sends the affliction for a reason, and it is to transform us.

THIRTY YEARS OF TEARS

The Lord put me through thirty years of affliction which I call my "thirty years of tears." I spent thirty years in the furnace of affliction. I prayed for it. I asked God to send me into the furnace of affliction, and so he did. I am not the same person who is coming out the other side of that furnace. I do not have anything like the pride I had before, and I did not know how proud I was before. Had the Lord confronted me, I would have denied all of it for I could not see it. We do not see what we do not want to see. But after thirty years in the furnace of affliction and with most of the pride burned out of me, now I can see what a difference it makes. All those resentments and all that unforgiveness, it gets burned out of you as well. And you feel a whole lot lighter. I am glad I do not have that U-Haul trailer filled with all that grief behind me anymore.

The key to the New Covenant is living in faith, hope and love, and letting God bring the birth of the life of Jesus Christ within our soul. The key to walking up right in the Lord is forgiveness and then the Lord will lead you into all truth. The problem is most of us are bound up in unforgiveness, lost in the rebellion of pride or snared with roots of bitterness. And that is when Satan comes along and tries to sell us a "new" alternative covenant.

MANY RELIGIOUS BUT NOT MANY RIGHTEOUS

Let us get real with each other. If you have a perfectly pure heart full of love, obedience and humility before the Lord, do you really think God cares what religious rituals you observe. The truth is, only people who repent from their hearts go to heaven, while the people who are caught up in all of these other religious arguments, for the most part, all go to hell. It is not about religious ritual. The Lord said "Go and learn what I mean by this, I prefer mercy over sacrifice."

We do not need to get religious, we need to become righteous. You do not need some man to tell you how to live a more religious life; you need to get in your prayer closet and do some business with the Lord. If Satan has strongholds in your life, areas in your soul that have been occupied by the enemy and now you have a compulsion to sin, then you need to fast and pray to break those off of you. The true weapons of our warfare are fasting and prayer. It is something we are all called to do. If you cannot fast, then try the Daniel fast of just a vegetarian diet for a season. Figure out what you can do. You can do it, and do it with all your heart, for you are doing it unto the Lord.

Jesus told us if we want to enter the kingdom we have to become as little children. What are the attributes of a little child? They love everybody, they do not have a lot of unforgiveness in their hearts, and they do not run around judging everybody.

DO YOU HAVE JESUS IN YOUR HEART

I had a friend whose four-year-old grandson was an evangelist and he loved to preach the word of God. Of course the only crowd he could preach to was his two-year-old sister. So he would tell her, "Sarah, do you know Jesus? Do you have Jesus in your heart?" Sarah would say "I don't know" in absolute terror but then turn around and say "but I love him" with a heart filled with total joy. That is the New Covenant. I love him, and he loves me. The New Covenant is all about walking in the Holy Spirit and walking out our faith in love. It is about walking out the will of God, and leaving your *I will* at the cross.

It is all about love. If I have not love, I am nothing. I have accomplished nothing without love, because God is love and everything God does through the Holy Spirit is a manifestation of his love. His faith and his hope and his love all come by the Holy Spirit, for the Spirit of God is the revelation of Jesus Christ.

The entire New Covenant is about being set free to walk in relationship with God. We cannot walk with the Lord in the dark counsel of the mind of the flesh. God already told us how we get there. We follow the footsteps of Jesus. We forgive everyone who has trespassed against us; we turn from the lust of the flesh and pick up our cross and walk with him in righteousness and let the Holy Spirit lead the way.

THE LORD ALONE WILL GUIDE HIS SHEEP

You do not need a man to guide you, for the Lord will guide you, and all you have to do is be true in your heart. If you play a game in the imagination of your mind, where you pretend to tell God the truth, and you pretend that you walk with God, and with everyone else you wear a mask of pretense, all you will accomplish with your religious façade is to fool yourself. People are fooling themselves, while they walk down the wide road to destruction. They are all pretenders, all walking in pretense. They are not honest with themselves, rather they are deceiving themselves. In the last days, evil men will wax worse and worse, deceiving and being deceived.

That is precisely what is happening in most churches today; we have been conditioned to hide at church, because there is no one you can trust. So, people get ensnared in the dark places of the earth, and then, the lying spirits come in with their flood of false doctrine, a virtual symphony of lies and deception. There are thousands of Christian deceptions, and most of the people get swept up by the one or more of them, but every one of them takes you away from the simplicity of the gospel of Jesus Christ. Repent and believe, and begin to walk in a love relationship with the Lord; the only requirement is you have to forsake your sins. You do not get to keep your sin, if you want to walk with him. And he commands you to forgive everyone, for if you want to be forgiven of everything, you must forgive everyone. If you don't, you won't.

SEEK HIM WITH ALL YOUR HEART

We must seek him with all of our hearts, all that matters is whether your heart is broken before the Lord and whether you are crying out from the bottom your heart because only then does God hear you, and only then does heaven respond. If you are praying in the intellectual quarters of your mind, it will be largely ineffective, but when you begin to pray from the broken parts of your heart, then God's heart is touched, and when God sees his children crying out and turning to him with all of their hearts, then heaven responds and the earth moves.

If we are merely playing a game we call church, pretending to be religious, while slandering each other because people do not match up to our little expectations, then we are doing the work of the evil one, and we have simply deceived ourselves. The reality is we may be one of the many who are lost among the congregation of the dead.

ALL ABOARD

So, it is all aboard for those who are coming aboard, because the remnant ship of true faith is about to set sail. And the rest of you, who want to stay within the outer court, filled with its compromise and sin, and continue to play your religious games, be advised: the Temple has been scheduled for burning again and where you are dwelling will be burnt to the ground soon and you will no doubt burn with it. In that final burning, and in that final place of affliction, which in your case will be in a literal furnace, all this nonsense will disintegrate right before your eyes. And you will be brought to the place of total repentance, and then God will hear you from heaven, and you will be healed and born again in the image of his Son and we will see you in the kingdom.

If you are so lost in your deceptions that you do not even know the Lord, then you will go the way of the many that are found on the wide road which leads only to destruction. All I can say to you is, I'm sorry; I prayed for you, and I tried to reach you, but obviously I cannot, so I will have to let you go now.

To the remnant that are being saved by the grace of God, I say God Bless you, and may you have God's speed because we are all about to go where no man has ever been before. So, batten down the hatches, and put your armor on. We are getting ready to walk into the Great Tribulation. It is time to get our garments ready, time to get all the spots out. It is also time to get your sword out, and make sure your lamp is full of Oil, for we are surely about to enter into the Great and Awesome Day of the LORD.

THE WAY OF HOLINESS

The ministry of Jesus Christ is the only way which leads to life. "And a highway shall be there, and a way and it shall be called *the way of Holiness*; the unclean shall not pass over it; but it shall be for those: the wayfaring men, though fools, shall not err therein. No lion shall be there, nor any ravenous beast shall go up thereon, it shall not be found there; but the redeemed shall walk there: and the ransomed of the LORD shall return, and come to Zion with songs and everlasting joy upon their heads: they shall obtain joy and gladness, and sorrow and sighing shall flee away." [93]

Only the ministry of Jesus, which is the very life of Jesus Christ, walked out in the spirit of love and truth, can ever lead us to true life, while all of the other ministries will find their end in Death Valley.

First Fruit

The Spirit of the Lord spoke through me, and his word was in my tongue. He that rules over men must be just, ruling in the fear of God. And he shall be as the light of the morning, when the sun rises, even a morning without clouds; as the tender grass springing out of the earth on a day of clear shining after rain. 2nd Samuel 23:2-4

For the earth shall bring forth fruit of herself; first the blade, then the ear, and after that the full corn in the ear. Mark 4:28

This chapter came forth as an audio teaching on the portal web site.[94] Readers may enjoy listening to the audio recording which is archived on the internet, under the title, *Search the Scriptures.*

I am the vessel which has been poured out; for God desires to use the weak things of this world to confound the strong, for only when we are weak, can he show himself strong within us.

The wisdom of God and the revelation of Scripture are so contrary to the way of our natural minds. We naturally believe we need to be strong, and the last thing we want is to become weak. And the very last thing we want, is to come to the end of ourselves. We have a survival instinct that causes us to just keep on keeping on with the works of the flesh; one more time around the mountain, one more attempt at doing it in our own strength and maybe, if we tell the same story one more time, it might finally become the truth. But it never does. The works of the flesh always produce the same bitter harvest, and they will always bring forth the same briars and thorns; and the best we can accomplish is just wood, hay and stubble. Whatever temporal value there was for the wood, and whatever limited life there may have been for the hay, that time is ending soon, for the time of the end of all flesh has finally come.

God has been giving his warnings to his people for many years that this time would come. The Spirit of God has been speaking to whoever would listen, warning that the days of ease are ending soon. Now, after so many years, we are finally here, and the Lord is now standing at the door, for the time which is called *summer* in the Scriptures is coming upon all of us very soon.

ALL THE PLANS OF THE ENEMY

In the summer of 2014, the Lord spoke to me: "Now that I have revealed to you all of the plans of the enemy, I am going to show you my plans to rebuild my house." The plans of the enemy which were revealed by the Lord are all laid out within the book, *The Day of the Lord is at Hand, Seventh Edition* and God's plan to rebuild his house is the focus of the seven volumes of *Search the Scriptures*. These are God's plans and not the plans of a man, and his plan begins with the matters of our heart that we might become a part of the First Fruit offering, which he has prepared as a present, and as a gift for his only begotten Son. The Father has been preparing this gift in secret, since before the world began.

We are entering a strange time, and I am in a strange place as I write these words. And things are really getting interesting now. Every day is an adventure with the Lord. When you are led by his spirit, he leads us into amazing things, and I am utterly amazed at all the things he is doing. One of the things that may seem a little strange is the Lord is bringing us back to the place of our origins.

The Lord has brought me back. As I work day and night on this book, I am working in exactly the same place where I first found the word of the Lord sixteen years ago. This is where my first book, *The Day of the Lord is at Hand,* was born. I do not even live in this state anymore and yet the Lord has brought me back to finish the seventh edition of *The Day of the Lord is at Hand* in the same place where it all began. It is in this same place, that I have also begun working on my new book, *Search the Scriptures*. Both of these books began in exactly the same place, only the name on the door in the beginning was Field Stone. It was a great and mighty company, and I was a laborer in that field. I was managing the pension money for that company and the investment portfolio for First Fruit, a private foundation belonging to the Lord. And it was here, in the early morning hours of each day that I prayed unto the Lord for almost a year about the stock market. And it was here that I was shown the judgment of God which is coming soon upon our nation, and which is the message of my first book, *The Day of the Lord is at Hand*.

These last few years have been quite amazing, for the Lord has blown away the field of stones, and all the stones have now been removed. The economic collapse which began in 2008 devastated the housing market along with the Field Stone Company; it no longer even exists in this state. And the only thing that has remained, which was here from the beginning, is First Fruit, for the Lord's portion cannot be burned in the fire.

I have been working in this field for over thirty years, and it was here, in a field of stones, that the Lord had hidden me away. But within that field, there was also the First Fruit of God hidden. And now that the Lord has removed the stones of stumbling, and has thrown aside the rocks of offense, he is making a way for his First Fruits to come forth. He has been clearing the ground so the First Fruits can arise in the day of clear shining that is coming soon. It will come in the time of the early rains and in the time when the corn begins to turn *aviv* in the spring. The early and the latter rains are going come together again in the early part of spring. The Scripture reveals before the day of the Lord begins, first must come a time for both the former and the latter rains, for they come together in spring, before the time of the end.

I want to share a prophecy with you, which I received in the beginning, because the ministry and the mission that God gave me with the book, *The Day of the Lord is at Hand,* is now coming to an end. Even as the hardened hearts and the stones of stumbling, which are rocks of offense, have been removed from the field, the burden of carrying the *Day of the Lord* is being lifted off of me. The book is going to be published in a seventh edition and that will be my final work on this message.

THE WORDS OF THE LORD
ARE PURIFIED SEVEN TIMES

The word of God is purified seven times. The reason God's word must be purified, is because it comes forth from out of impure vessels. It is not that God's word is imperfect, but it needs to be cleansed from the fingerprints of the men that brought it forth. "The words of the LORD are pure words: as silver tried in a furnace of earth, they are purified seven times."[95] So the book, *The Day of the Lord is at Hand* has now been cleansed seven times, and it is now a complete and perfected work. Now it is ready for the eternal purpose for which it was intended.

We need to decrease and the presence of the Lord to increase within us. And the word that came forth from the Spirit needs to be separated from the chaff. In so many ways, and in every little detail, the Lord is purifying this word. Even the picture on the cover is now a perfectly clear blood red moon. It has been purified, whereas with the original cover, an error was made by the printer and they fogged up the moon, a picture of a work that had not yet been purified.

I rejoice that *The Day of the Lord is at Hand* has been published in a seventh edition. But I am also very happy to be reassigned if you will, to now labor to bring forth a word for the equipping of the saints. *The Day of the Lord* is a prophetic warning of what is coming upon America, and a warning of what is coming upon the church. But it is also a message of hope, because it outlines the deliverance plan which God has prepared for his remnant. At the same time it is still a very heavy word. It has awakened a lot of people to righteousness. The Lord has used it to save many people, and to bring the prodigals back. But at the same time, people need equipping. I need equipping. We all need to be equipped, for the journey that lays before us, and that is the purpose of *Search the Scriptures*. The volumes of this book are designed to break the yokes of evil one off of the lives of the remnant of God, and designed to bring victory and deliverance to his people.

The Lord himself is bringing forth this word. I can tell you at the moment, my brain is blurred. I started working this morning at 3 AM, and that is not really early for me, because I have been getting up at 3 AM for the last three months and it has finally caught up with me. After three months, I finally got tired and my whole body and mind has collapsed, but praise God that means something good is coming forth tonight, for there is nothing that can come out of me.

THE FIELD OF STONES

I was given a prophecy entitled *The Field of Stones* right after *The Day of the Lord is at Hand* came out of the field of stones in 1998. Those who read the book may remember the epilogue in which I talk about the parable of the steward who found the great treasure in the Field of Stone. It was in the Field of Stones that this treasure was found. Praise God!

This is the prophetic word that was given to me in 1998: "Many of you are weary, for you have labored removing stones from fields that you were never assigned to, and you have become exhausted. And now you are tempted to fall asleep, right before the time of the harvest. The Lord would say to you, arouse yourself, shake off the dust and stand up and look around, there is another field over the hill that has been rightly prepared for you."

"The time of the harvest has come, and it is a time of entering in, and it is a time of redemption and a time of restoration, and a time of entering into the fruit of those who labored before you. For the time of the harvest is the time of the reaping, where you will reap that which you have not sown, and experience the reward of those who arrived late to labor but yet they shall share in a full reward. But beware the Field of Stones, for this is a land of hardened hearts and the Lord himself will deal with this earth. Cross over into the prepared field, the one that has been properly staked out for you and measured by the Lord's hand, and allotted as the land of your portion and the land of your anointing. For therein the rows are measured according to each harvester's pace and there is joy in this field and not burden. So lay down the false burdens, before they lay you down, for many are carrying a rock of stumbling, and a stone of offense and it is time to lay down the stones that the Lord has not called us to carry." Praise God! We don't have to remain in a field of stones, and we no longer have to carry the false burdens anymore.

WE SHALL ALL BE CHANGED

We are entering into a season of change. I know God is changing me dramatically, and I sure love the work that he is doing. I am confident he is changing you as well. We have been patient; we have been waiting and praying. And we have been fasting and preparing our hearts. We have been faithfully calling on his name, studying his word, and many of us have been seeking him with all of our hearts, doing whatever we knew to do.

It has been a long wait for some of us. And for some, the burdens have been heavy, but the Lord has heard our prayers. He has heard your prayers and God says I have seen your tears.

And I have captured them in the palm of my hand and I will not let them fall to the ground, for your hearts are precious to me, and I am coming to set you free. The Lord is coming to reveal himself; and he is coming to visit his house. He is coming to us first, and he is coming to clean his house.

He warned us when he said to me "summer is coming soon, tell the people to clean their houses." So I think he has given us a little clue on when he is going to come and visit you. We have a little season of time to make our final preparations, so let us sweep the house clean, and remove all the leaven from every room. Let us do the work of uprooting the giants and redeeming the land within our souls because we have the victory, it is ours to receive, and no one can take it from us, or stop us from entering in, only we ourselves. We are the only people in all of creation who can stop the plan of God in our lives. No demon in hell, no power on this earth, and no other person alive today can stop us from entering in, for the Lord has placed before each of us, an open door and he bids us to come. He bids us to prepare ourselves for his visitation, but we must follow the Master in his ways, and we must prepare our hearts according to the specifications of his word; for our hearts must begin to line up with the word of God.

There is nothing we can do to change the past. That which is past is past, and that which is lost is lost. Now for some of us, the Lord is going to restore things unto us; things that were stolen from us. God is going to restore them, but first He must do a work within us, and that work involves his plumb line.

GOD IS LOOKING FOR THE TRUTH

He is looking to measure the truth. God is calling us to come out from the shadows. He is calling us to have courage and be of good cheer; to stand in our faith, step out of the boat, and walk on the water. He is calling us to walk above the sea of humanity, where the nations are drowning in their lies. And therein lies the reason for their death, because they would not come out of the lie. The Lord is calling his remnant to come out of the shadows and be fearless, be of good courage, for he is with you. But God is looking for the truth. Jesus said "I am the way, the truth and the life" and the doorway is the truth. The way of the holy and righteous remnant is the way of truth, and we have to embrace the truth, we have to become the truth, and be willing to leave our reputation behind.

We must be willing to forsake our pride, and lay the axe to the root of that abominable tree. We must be willing to step out of the shadows now. We have been hiding ourselves. Many people are hiding in shadows, because they are afraid, and they are hiding for fear that someone might see. And in some of us that hiding is so deep, we have actually hidden from ourselves a part of our personality, in which there are things buried which the Lord desires, he insists even, that they be removed from our lives.

There are issues of fear, memories filled with shame, and things of the flesh that are buried deep within, and God wants to bring them out so that he may set us free. And the truth is the way. We not only must know the truth, we must have the courage to speak the truth! Find the truth, and when you finally embrace the truth, sell everything you own, and "buy the truth and sell it not."

Forsake everything to find the treasure in the field, which is the true word of God. And in order to have the true word of God within you, you must have the truth within you. Because if you have lies hidden within and you try to take the word of God upon yourself, and eat the bread of life, the living manna, which comes out of heaven, you will only deceive yourself. If you have not removed the lies from within your soul, those dark habitations of the earth, the places of cruelty, where bondage and sins yet remain, will deceive you and you will be unable to see out of the darkness within you.

If you remain in these dungeons of darkness which are the places of guilt and shame, you will be afraid that if you come into the light, everyone will see your shame. But those are all lies from the enemy. The Lord says "No, my people will not be ashamed." If you come into the light, the Lord will clothe you with his robes of righteousness. If you have the faith and the courage to obey your God, he will remove the strongholds of the evil one from your life. It is through the truth that God is going to begin to bring the restoration of your life.

God has been ministering to me about the truth, as I have been working on the Dark Counsel chapter of *Out of the Darkness*, which calls us to come out of the lie, and out of the shadows, and out of that place where we were in denial. For this is the key to entering into the true secret hiding place of the Most High God. Because it is not in the shadows, you cannot find it in the darkness, and you cannot enter the narrow way with these things still hidden within. We must embrace the truth, and I know in my life, I had lies I did not even know about. I could not even see them. I thought I had the truth; I had it as far as I could see it. I was trying to measure with the plumb line in my hand, and some of the lines were straight, but not all of them.

I could not see the crookedness, but the Lord took the veil off my eyes and he showed me these areas in which there were lies, of which I was utterly unaware. At first I did not want to even believe it and so I cried out "No Lord, it can't be true" but God said "It is true, and there is more."

THE FAVOR OF THE LORD

This is the central issue with the remnant, but how do you get into the remnant? How do you come under the favor of Almighty God so that you will be protected when so much judgment will be poured out, that you would be hidden away in the heart of God, in an hour of tribulation such as has never been, and when the end of all flesh comes upon the earth. How do you find the secret hiding place of the Most High God?

Well it is not through pretending, and many of us have become very skilled at pretending. Some of us even became confused, thinking that it was faith, believing if we just pretend long enough, and believe that the pretense is real, something magical is going to happen, and God is going to turn our lies into the truth. But that is not what the Scripture teaches. God does not turn our lies in the truth; our lies remain lies for as long as we hold onto them and hide them within our hearts. But when we have the courage, when we trust Jesus enough to obey him, and when we no longer care about protecting our reputations, or fear that we might have something to lose, and are no longer concerned that it might hurt a little, then we will finally embrace the truth, and we will finally be ready to let the truth come out of us.

I am ready, and maybe it is a little easier for me. The Lord made it easy for me, because he burned my life utterly in the flames and everything that I had was consumed in the fires, so that all I had left was ashes. I did not have to fear losing anything, for everything was already lost. The Lord put me through the purging process, to where I actually began to enjoy the pain, not for the purpose of the pain. No, it certainly was uncomfortable, but because of the holiness I began to feel within. It was growing, and it was beginning to capture my entire heart and I wanted more of it. It was worth more than the pain, and so I began to cry out "Lord more! I love your threshing floor Almighty God. Lord more, and don't stop until it's done." So I no longer fear the pain, the pain is our friend and I have nothing left to lose, and I also no longer fear being discovered, for the Lord has already discovered me to myself.

The Lord said to me recently "why are you concerned with what the other people think, in the end they think only of themselves." It doesn't really matter if we get discovered, the people do not even think about us anyway. In the end, they will be thinking only of themselves and their end is coming very quickly now. As for us, it is the truth that is going to set us free.

I am going to have some conversations with some people that I wounded. I did not even see the things that I did at the time, but the Lord showed them to me, and now I see them. These are people I love, more than my own life. I am going to have some conversations with some of my family, and I am going to tell them the truth.

I do not know why most families do not speak the truth to one another. Maybe you were blessed to come from a family that always told the truth, but many of us came from families where nothing that deep or serious was ever discussed. Not that everyone overtly lied to one another, we just conveniently never discussed those painful issues; we left them in the shadows, with all of those hurtful feelings of shame and despair, and all the broken hearts and never discovered them, never brought them into the light.

And in so doing, we have given such an advantage to Satan, because we left our loved ones wondering what really happened. We would not talk about those deep hurtful things, so we let all the other people to wonder, and the enemy was right there tell them all sorts of lies. People feel rejected because of our behavior, in which we hurt them deeply and we did not even see what we were doing. They feel very much rejected, but the truth is, we love them very much. But unless we are willing to tell them, how would they know?

A NATION OF PEOPLE AFRAID OF THE TRUTH

Everywhere they go, they hear nothing but lies; a whole world drowning in lies, and a nation of people afraid of the truth. The apostates are afraid of the truth, for theirs is only a counterfeit covenant, a covenant with death, and it will not cover them on the Day of Judgment. Choosing a false covenant, they too will one day die. But ours is a covenant of life, engraved for all of time, in the blood of our God. And He is the truth, and if there is one thing that is the key to coming out of the deceptions, and coming out of the bondage, coming out of the battle that many of us seem to be losing, it is the truth.

In this I have a bit of an advantage. I am not afraid of the truth and I have nothing that I fear being discovered about me, because I have already seen it all. And I know the same sin, the same disease is actually found in all of us, but we have the Savior, we have the blood of the Lord. We need not fear our sin, if we are ready to forsake it, we need not fear bringing it into the light; that is what is going to release it. We should be afraid of hiding it in our tents, because it is going to be discovered in the day of visitation. The Lord already knows, for there is nothing hidden from him.

We should not fear the truth, because it is the truth that sets us free. If we refuse to tell the truth, then we will remain in bondage, and will continue to give the enemy the advantage over us and our families. As far as the truth producing a little pain, well maybe it is pain that is good. The Scripture says that Jesus learned obedience from the things he suffered, and suffering is a very real part of salvation; it is the reason why God chose us in a furnace of affliction, and the reason why we need to fast and pray.

Suffering works into us the knowledge of righteousness and the fear of the Lord, and brings us into reality so that we may see the flesh for what it is. The Lord learned righteousness and obedience through the things that he suffered. Now, in him was no sin, and he is the Holy One, the eternal Son of God, but he also took on the form of a man. He became a man, even though he is the eternal King, and the forever Blessed Son, the only Son of the Father; nevertheless he became a man and he walked among us. He became as one of us, even though he is our God; and as a man he learned, and as a man he grew in favor with

God and men. He learned obedience through the things he suffered.

Our generation is the first generation that has been able to avoid, to a great extent, most of the pain and suffering endured in previous generations. We go to the dentist and they administer Novocain. We go to the doctor and he gives us pain killers. The Lord appoints unto us suffering, and we take pain killers, and we short-circuit the process; maybe that is why so few of us have learned obedience to the truth, maybe we have cheated ourselves.

I had an experience with obedience learned through suffering this week. I went to a Dentist and I thought I had a small problem with a tooth. It turned out the entire root had broken and the dentist had to do an emergency extraction. The tooth once had a root canal, so the roots had been replaced with cement. The tooth broke off as they tried to extract it. Only the roots remained, and the dentist who originally put them in, actually drilled one of them into my jaw bone. They had to pull out the roots and when they removed them, they ripped out part of my jawbone. At that moment, I went over the moon. I thought, "Lord, I don't know how you endured the cross." I had only experienced a little bit of his suffering, and it was beyond the moon for me; it was a taste of the cross, for it went all the way into the bone.

THEY PIERCED MY HANDS AND FEET

Having his bones pierced. That is the price Jesus paid for us and I will tell you, that few minutes of pain, really put the fear of God in me, and I already feared the Lord because I have already had a truckload of pain; but that gave me a measure of what the cross must have been like. That was a whole new world, my friends. The Lord held us in his hands on the cross as he endured that world in its infinity. What he did for us, I do not have words to describe, but I know one thing, he asks us to come out of the darkness, and to have courage, and not to be afraid of the shame, because there is power in confessing your sins one to another. The Lord wants to deliver you. You have been praying and praying, and asking and asking, and God is answering your prayers, but it is going to require a step of faith.

There are requirements in the issues of the kingdom. It is by his grace that we were freely loved and through which mercy was extended to us. And his grace and mercy is free, but our salvation is not free. We have to repent and forsake our sins. We have to pick up our cross and deny ourselves. We have to find the truth, and then we have to "buy the truth and sell it not." And we have to find the courage to obey the Lord. Some of the things the Lord asks us to do are a little scary to us. It is not like the Lord is asking us to actually endure anything as severe as His cross, but we are afraid.

THE DECEPTION OF PRIDE

We are afraid it might hurt a little emotionally, and afraid we might be discovered for the frauds that we really all are, because in our flesh, we are all frauds and we are all pretenders. And in our flesh, we are all full of ourselves, immature, and bound up in the sin of pride. We are lost in our deceptions where we are more than happy to fashion a religious robe of the righteousness in our flesh, so we can sing loud on Sunday. All the while we are yet hiding the true nature of our sin, which is the pride and rebellion which remains within. And it is out of our pride that we resist confessing our sins one to another. And it is rebellion before God that we would even choose to stand in pride.

For what are we proud? Why do we stand in pride? What deeds have we done? Is our knowledge so great that we choose to remain puffed up? We do not know as we should have known. No, it is nothing more than a deception. To the degree that we are proud, that is the degree to which we are deceived.

Pride can only exist within you to the degree of the deception of sin within your heart. And the deception of sin can only exist within you, to the degree that you have shadows within. The only way you can have shadows within your heart is if you have idols and graven images that are still standing, and they are blocking out some of the light. They are casting a shadow over part of your heart, and we need to remove them, and we all have them. So do not let Satan tell you that you will be rejected. There is not a one of us that does not have them. The Lord told me "You have all fallen from the truth" and when he says "all" he means all. Ours is a backslidden generation, in which the best of us is worthless and the most upright among us, are sharper than a thorn hedge. And the only ones, who are seeking the Lord in true humility, are the broken hearted and afflicted ones. But the Lord wants to restore his people and He wants all of this darkness out of our lives.

GOD IS READY TO RESTORE

We have been praying and praying, and asking God to move, and he is ready to move. And we have been asking God for deliverance, and deliverance is at the door. We have been asking the Lord for the restoration of our families and God is ready to restore. But it is the things that we are afraid to bring out into the light, that are holding back all of heaven's blessings. On occasion the Lord lets me listen into the conversations in the camp of the enemy. I am not sure why he does this, I guess probably so I could tell you, but from time to time, I have been able to hear conversations that have been occurring in hell as Lucifer gives instructions to his principalities. Recently he said to them "It is a good thing they're still proud. We've been saved by their pride many times. Otherwise we would have had to give back to them everything we've stolen."

Your pride is only a friend to your enemy. It is saving and preserving the strongholds of the evil one in your life. The faster you humble yourself and cut that tree down, the faster you will be set free. Hit it at the roots, kill the roots and pull them out of the ground. There is nothing more effective to cutting out the tree of pride then to go to your loved ones and friends with whom you have an offence, and where you need to seek reconciliation, and humble yourself, and tell them the truth.

THE COMMANDMENT OF THE LORD

Some of us have some pretty severe things to deal with, but we need to open and honest and not hold back anything. We need to bring everything into the light and not hide anything anymore. We cannot afford to care about protecting our reputations. We must stop worrying about what we might lose. The truth is, for all of us, we are not going to lose anything when we obey the Lord, when we finally bring this junk forward. The only one who is going to lose is Satan; he is going to lose his advantage over you, and he is going to lose the ground that he has in you. And he is going to lose the ability to hold back your blessings, and then he is going to lose everything he stole from you, because it is going to be given back to you by the commandment of the Lord.

So, rather than hesitating in these measures, understand children, tremendous blessings await you. Rather than being afraid, you should be rejoicing. So we need to be praying for the truth, searching our heart with the plumb line of God's word, and diligently fasting and praying. We need to ask the Lord, what truth do I need in me, and where are the lies hidden within, for these lies are all part of the Dark Counsel within.

The Lord took the Dark Counsel message, which he brought forth two years ago, and he has added some wonderful truth to the pages of this book. And this really is a book which came forth from the Lord. I am just a bookkeeper, and an accountant who keeps some books for the Lord. I keep the books for the First Fruits of the Lord and these books are the First Fruit of the redeemed of the Lord. And they are not coming forth out of a field of stones, for the stones have all been cleared away. These messages are coming forth out of a field full of the First Fruits of God. Praise God, but first, we are going to have to break a few things. We are going to have to break our pride, and we are going to have to break out of our fear.

Fear is the central power of the kingdom of darkness. We are going to have to overcome our fears and begin to trust the Lord. And if we break a few eggs, we will simply make an omelet. Maybe those things need to break. Maybe we will break a few hearts, but maybe those hearts are hardened, and once they are broken, through our steps of faith, God's healing can come in. But we must come out of the fear. As you embrace the truth, and I mean totally, the fear will suddenly begin to lose place within you, and there will be no more torment.

I know dark days are coming upon us, and very soon. I received a real-world confirmation a few days go through my business. Things are occurring on a very large scale that are consistent with an eminent collapse. Powerful people are making very dramatic moves that only make sense if we are almost out of time. But we already knew this had been confirmed, and that the time of fear is coming soon upon the earth. The whole world shall soon become afraid and the hypocrites will also become terrified, for the generation of his wrath is about to be confronted with the judgment of Almighty God.

OUR LIVES BELONG TO THE LORD

If we still have fear hidden in our hearts, we will be very tempted to become afraid along with them, so we have to get fear out of our lives. We have got to get it out, and we have to develop an immunity to it. Our lives belong to the Lord, assuming you have given your entire life to him; your life is now the property of the Lord. You have nothing to fear, you do not even have a problem, for your life has become the concern of the Lord. We need to stop worrying about saving ourselves, saving our reputations, and shielding ourselves from the pain. The suffering is here for a reason, and if we have to go through a season of suffering, we should understand that it was appointed unto us that we could learn righteousness and obedience.

We need to do the things the Lord is telling us to do; even if we are afraid, even if we are not comfortable, even if our flesh is screaming "I don't want to." Do it anyway. Do it out of obedience, because of what Jesus did for you. He did not want those nails piercing his bones. The pain of the cross, I cannot even imagine the intensity of it, and He could have come down off that cross at any time. He could have stopped that at any time, the only thing that would have happened is that he would have had to let go of you. That's all. If he just let you go, he could have stopped all of his pain and suffering. But you would have slipped out of his hand right into hell, so He was never going to let go of you. He endured all of the suffering of the cross to save us. And we are afraid of our reputations being wounded a little?

A TIME FOR THE SURVIVORS TO LAMENT

Who cares? Once that is gone, it is just one less thing you do not have to trouble yourself with. Fine, let's all be of no reputation now. I honestly cannot think of anything good any of us have done any way, besides what was done through the Holy Spirit. But we are all worried about a little pain, okay; we probably need it. And we are worried we might lose something. Are you kidding me? You are about to lose everything. We need to take very seriously the things the Lord is saying to us, because a time of unbelievable woe will soon be revealed unto mankind, that word *woe* means a time of crying, and of lamentations and of weeping, of wailing and of grieving and mourning, and it will be a time for the survivors to lament.

And this time is upon us now. We are headed right into it, and we do not need our pride, or to be afraid, and we do not need to miss the Lord in this hour if we are to be a part of his remnant. So we have to take the tough steps. We cannot be the virgins who awaken to find they have no oil in their lamps. And believe me there are a lot of people with no oil in their lamps; and there are a lot of people walking around today in a spiritual state of sleep. They are sleeping in Sodom, while they are dreaming that they are walking in Zion, and they think they are somehow in the remnant because they figured out what time it is.

Listen, the unbelievers have also figured out what time it is. Everybody that is awake to any degree knows what time it is. If you do not have oil in your lamps, it is not going to matter. Your knowledge of what time it is will not save you. The disciples all fell asleep in the garden, even three times, until finally in frustration the Lord told them "go back to sleep." This is a prophetic picture of the time we are living in.

And that was also a prophetic utterance which the Lord spoke to the church, and to his people, and it has been fulfilled in this hour. Most of the church is asleep in their hearts, and some are even sleeping while reading this book. But God desires to wake us up, and when we get a taste of the cross and when it goes to the bone, we will wake up.

WE MUST HAVE OIL IN OUR LAMPS

And when the knock at the door occurs at four in the morning, you will also wake up. When the soldiers came to arrest Jesus, the disciples all woke up. But for the remnant, now is the time for us to wake up; we must awaken, because we must be filled with the oil. We must have oil in our lamps, because the Bridegroom is coming soon. He has already warned us. The other sleeping virgins have not been warned. At least we know he is coming, and we know "heaven is expecting now." The Lord spoke those words to me a few months back, and the Lord is getting ready to come, and wake up all of the virgins and *we know* his coming is nigh.

So, we should do everything in our power to make sure our lamps are full of oil in this hour. That is really all that matters now. Forget the pride thing. We should not even care about our pride anymore. The whole world is going to be changed soon and no one is going to care about your pride. No one is going to care about your ruined reputation either. No one is going to care about any of these things, because in the end, they will only think of themselves. And for the vast majority of them, the end will be upon them before they even know it. So we need to deal with the issues that pertain to the end of our preparations, so that we may become part of the First Fruit offering of the Lord.

God has been so good; he is so good to all of us. I am speechless that the Lord would save me in this hour. With so many asleep, why am I awake? Why is God speaking to me? I honestly do not know. The Lord even asked me that question; "Do you know why I speak to you like this?" I was honest and I said "No Lord, I really don't." God is having mercy where he chooses to have mercy. And praise the Lord, we are among his little flock. But we have to do our part.

I am a zealot, and I am a little bit intense; and maybe some people cannot handle that. But where we are going is about to become very intense, and what is coming upon our nation is going to be very intense indeed. During the history of Israel, when the intense days came upon the nation, the people from the tribe of Benjamin became very popular. We all need to get intense now, which means we need to give a hundred percent. We do not just try halfway. We go for it with everything we got. The one thing the Lord has really impressed on me, in this little window of time, particularly as I have been working on the chapter *Dark Counsel*, is this whole issue of the truth.

The Lord is so good, he tells us exactly what we need to do, but we have to get real now. Some of you may already be past this issue, and if that is you, then perhaps there will be something in the balance of this message for you. But a lot of saints are not yet done. They have not finished with the issue of cleansing their hearts of all of the stuff that has been buried in there for a very long time.

It is the truth that is going to get it out and restore relationships. Satan comes along and tells us, if we bring it all into the light, the people are going to reject us, we might lose some relationships, and people might get offended. But the opposite is what is going to happen.

I WANT TO TELL YOU THE TRUTH

People are going to be blessed by the truth. I am going to make sure that all my friends and family know the truth because I am going to sit down with them and say "I want to tell you the whole truth." How often does anybody come up to you and say "I want to tell you the whole truth." When do we ever even get the truth in this world? How many times do we even go and tell the truth, and how common is the truth?

Everybody greets each other and asks "How you are?" "I'm fine." That's great, we are all fine except were all in deep trouble too. If you do not think your deep trouble, then you do not understand the reality you are facing. Or maybe you are already in the secret hiding place of the Most High God. If that is you, then you are not in deep trouble, but there are a lot of people around you that are in very deep trouble now. We need to focus on them. There are a whole lot of people still living in a garbage dump spiritually, and they still have all of the trash of the Dark Counsel still very much alive in them.

The orphaned children from the *Answer the Call International*[96] ministry in India were all living in the garbage dump, literally. They were homeless orphans, but they were Christians; little boys and girls, living in the streets of the Third World, digging through the garbage to survive. They prayed and the Lord intervened and pulled them out of the garbage dump. They are little prayer warriors. When you live in a garbage dump, and you beg for food, and you dig through garbage every day for something to eat, and pray to Jesus for help, and then Jesus intervenes, and he pulls you out of the garbage, you become a prayer warrior. These little guys are prayer warriors, and they pray constantly. They pray before they do anything. These little kids know that there are Christians in America that are helping them, and they storm heaven for the blessing of the people that are blessing them.

DO NOT BE AFRAID

The Lord pulled me out of the garbage dump once too, so maybe that is why I care so much about these little kids living in the garbage dumps of the Third World. The Lord pulled me out of the garbage, and then he woke me from my sleep, when he showed me what is now coming. And then he called me to write the book, *The Day of the Lord is at Hand*. It was born within the offices of Field Stone. It literally came forth in their midst. In one of the company meetings I stood up and declared the word of God: "The Lord God Almighty is standing now, ready to judge, the entire earth." So they know the message.

I was fired for sharing the word of the Lord, when I stood up at their meeting. I was leading the meeting as the Director of Investments, and the Lord spoke audibly to me saying, "I wish to speak to this people." When I got home the Lord told me, "They are going to fire you, but do not be afraid, for you are not getting fired, you are being delivered." So I thought, I am going to lose my job, but who cares, I am being delivered, so who needs a job. And so I got fired. But they didn't really fire me, for they brought me back as a consultant, and I am still sitting here in the same office building in December of 2014.

I worked on *The Day of the Lord is at Hand* in this same building sixteen years ago. The stones of stumbling have now all been blown away, but I am still working for First Fruit, which has remained in the same exact location. And now I am working on my new book, *Search the Scriptures*, in the same place as before. Only now the name on the door is *First Fruit*. I am very excited to see what God is about to do with this book. Only God can do these things. *Search the Scriptures, Vol. I Out of the Darkness* was born within the same offices where *The Day of the Lord is at Hand* had come forth sixteen years ago.

The irony of all of this is they threw me out for the last time once the seventh edition of *The Day of the Lord is at Hand* was completed. I suppose they really do not want to hear the word of the Lord in this place anymore. And so, they asked me to leave once again. Only this time, I do not think I will be coming back. And very soon, there will be nothing to come back too.

We all must go forward on the path of the Lord's choosing, and that path leads us straight to the cross. The devil wants to stop us from going the way of the cross, and he wants to stop us from choosing only the truth. And if he can get us to hide anything at all, if he can get us to just shrink back, to not get out of the boat, and not take that step of faith, that is all he has to do, and he can keep us all stuck right where we are.

From my perspective, based on my knowledge of what is going on out there, there are very few of us that want to stay where we are right now. And for some of us, staying where we are right now is the most dangerous thing we could do.

SUMMER IS COMING SOON

As I wrote earlier, the Lord woke me from my sleep a few weeks ago, shouting that "summer is coming soon, tell the people to clean their houses." His voice was as loud as 110 decibels. I cannot yell as loud as the thunder of God's voice now coming forth from heaven. We all have to move fast now; and most of us need to move forward with the Lord on the issues in this book, for we must all come out of the darkness. Some of us also need to move physically to a new location, for the time of the heathen, and the reign of the dark ones, is about to begin. It is coming upon the whole earth very soon.

We must move forward with the Lord; we have to, because many of us are not ready for what is coming. But God wants to help us, so we need to step out in faith and face the fears that have been ruling over us all these years, because these fears have ruined us. We have to become the people who go and seek reconciliation. We have to become the people who restore our neighbors; we have to become the people to forgive first. And it does not matter what the other people did; it is all about getting the garbage out of us. The battle of our faith is really being fought over the issues of love in our life. That is the real battle, and the only battle worth winning now.

ALL THAT MATTERS

It all comes down to the love of the truth within the relationships which the Lord has given us. Those are the only things worth winning. Nothing else matters. It does not matter who ends up with the gold, or who does the visible job or who does things the Lord asked be done in the background. It does not matter. All that matters is that we are about our Master's business, and that we are faithful to him in the task to which we have been assigned.

And one of the tasks we have been assigned is to be a witness for the Lord, in our little universe, in our circle of friends, within our families and with our loved ones. And we desperately need to bring forth the anointing, the healing, and the restoration because God is planning on doing a major restoration work in his people.

Love covers a multitude of sins, and when you are willing to reach out and love the people around you, it covers a multitude of sins. So does the lack of love not cover sin? If love covers, what does the absence of love do? And what happens to a generation whose hearts have grown cold, and what will become of the *many* who are going to become offended soon, as the persecution is about to begin. We are going to be in the Day of the Lord soon, most likely by the end of the next year. That is my opinion, but I have been wrong before, so you could just ignore me once again, but it would be better to get ready and be one year early rather than one day late.

I do not think we are ready, and being ready is more than just talking about these issues. We have all heard some great teachings. We have all listened to some great words about the renewing of our minds through the washing of the word, and through the knowledge of the word. Those are all wonderful blessings from the Lord, but we are at the point where we have got to begin and step out and do the hard work of faith by living it out. We have to redeem the areas of our souls, which are not yet redeemed. We have got to do it by facing our fears.

We need to use faith, hope and love, to search out the truth. Jesus bore the pain of the cross and it went all the way to his bone. He already went through hell for us, to save us, because we are his prized possession. He is going to be with us when we step out, but we have got to step out in faith.

The church is one of the places where we were called to love one another, but how do we do that if we are afraid to tell each other the truth. We have to tell each other the truth. The whole issue comes down to the question of what are we going to believe, and it is not our words that matter, it is how we live out the truth in our hearts. We can say we believe in the truth, but if in our hearts, we let the fear hold us back, we are really placing more faith in the fear.

And fear is just one more part of the lie. The truth is we have nothing to fear from obeying the Lord. We also have nothing to fear from what is coming in the earth, and we have nothing to fear from what the men could do to us either. The only thing that we should fear is the Lord. Then you can laugh at the tribulation, and when these events come to pass, when everyone else is becoming terrified, you will be filled with peace.

THE PRESENT

As I was readying to leave on a recent ministry trip, I awoke in the morning and said "Good morning Lord." I thought to ask him: "Lord, how are you today?" Then I thought that is a dumb thing to ask the Lord, so I did not say it. But later it turned out from the conversation I had with the Lord that day, that it might not have been a dumb thing to ask him after all. That really surprised me. But I did not ask Lord "how are you today" instead I said "Lord, are you getting excited about your present? You have a present coming, and I know you know what it is. But I was just wondering if you are getting excited, because you are going to get your present soon."

The Scripture speaks of the present the Lord is about to receive: "In that time shall the present be brought unto the LORD of hosts of a people scattered and peeled, and from a people terrible from their beginning hitherto; a nation meted out and trodden under foot, whose land the rivers have spoiled, to the place of the name of the LORD of hosts, the mount Zion."[97]

The Lord has waited two thousand years for this present; I have had to wait for presents, but I have never waited that long for anything. I was just kind of curious, so I was asking the Lord, "are you getting excited." And then I said "Lord I am very excited about your present!" I am actually very excited about his present, which is why I am so excited about my little orphans in India, because they are part of his present. And I am going to help gift wrap some of the presents for the Lord. Some of us are part of this present too, because the present that will be given to the Lord, is the Holy Remnant, after they have been cleaned and purified and made perfect in Him.

THE HOLY REMNANT SHALL BE HIS

This little Holy Remnant, which Father God has prepared from before the foundation of the world, and who will be preserved from the fire, they are *The Present* which will soon be presented to the Lord.

I was merely wondering if the Lord was looking forward to it, because I did not know. I was just thinking in my own little terms, and I was getting excited, because God was going to get his present. How many times has Jesus gotten a present really? I think this is the first one, and maybe the only one he gets too. And he might have done all of this for one very special reason, which is more important to him than anything else.

The most important thing in his heart, could be this present, so to me, it seems like a really big deal. So, I was asking the Lord about his present, and then he started to talk to me about the present. But he talked about a lot of presents, and I had no idea that the gifts we bring to God are so important to the Lord and so important to us as well, for the gifts that we receive from God, are measured by the gifts that we give.

It turns out, some people did not give God very good gifts at all, and some did not give him anything. Some were just barren branches, that bore no fruit; and those branches are about to be cut off, and burned in the fire now. And some of the other branches bore rotten fruit, and fruit that was spoiled and it was no longer good and in fact it was poisonous fruit, which had the mixture of poisonous sin within. That fruit was actually bad, it was very bad fruit, like bad figs, and they were very bad, like the figs which the Lord talks about in the book of Jeremiah.

He is not happy with bad fruit, and he is not happy with barren branches either. And some of the people even gave the Lord offerings and presents, but they gave to the Lord from out of their leftovers. They spent all of their time and all of their money on their own pleasures, and then when they were done, if they had anything left over, only then would they bring an offering to him.

I GAVE MY PEOPLE EVERYTHING

He told me, "I gave my people everything, and I always put them first" but "some of them only give me of their leftovers." That is pretty heavy, and it makes me feel very sad. Then he said "some of my people don't even come at all." They do not even come and they do not even care to give him anything at all!

Here I was just inquiring about whether the Lord was getting excited about the present he is about to get, and he starts speaking about things I did not know anything about, and I started to wonder because some of his presents were *junkie presents.* This was my word, not God's, but they were presents that were no longer any good at all, and when you hear the whole message on *The Present,* you will understand about the *junkie gifts* because he said to me "I've received many presents and some of them were just like some of yours." I thought to myself, God has gotten presents like some of mine?

I didn't understand, but I got some *junkie presents* given to me and I didn't really get the connection at first, but some of us give junkie gifts to each other, and we give rotten fruit to each other too. Some of us do that all the time. And sometimes we have no fruit at all. Sometimes we don't even show up for each other. And the most amazing thing, the most astonishing thing, is the Lord takes this more seriously than I ever dreamed.

HOW WE TREAT EACH OTHER

This whole issue of how we treat each other is more important to the Lord than I ever imagined, and it hurts him when we hurt each other, or when we dishonor each other. We give each other rotten fruit, and think nothing of it, but God takes it personally. He owns the whole earth, and all of the people are his too, and what you are doing to the least of those that belong to him, he takes it personal, as if you did it to him. And I mean really personal. I had no idea, but it is important what we do for the Lord, and how we treat each other.

There is nothing that is closer to the heart of the Lord, than the care of his little children. We all have a natural empathy for children, especially for the little children; we have an instinct within us to protect them, and to help them, because they need it. They need us. The adults have to take care of the children or they are not going to make it. The Lord put that in our hearts because that is how he feels.

He has a special affinity for the children, because they are so helpless, and they are so innocent. They have not given him any junkie presents yet and they have not born any rotten fruit either. They have never been fruitless branches and they never fail to show up for the Lord, and they never give him the leftovers either, so they have not offended the Lord like some older Christians have, which I did not realize, but it turns out that is true.

Some of us have offended the Lord. Well, we better fix that right quick. And one of the ways we could fix that is by showing mercy to the poor and by helping widows and orphans and there is nothing more important than helping widows and orphans who are believers and who belong to the Lord. For in their hour of need, they have been crying out to him, and it matters a whole lot to the Lord, who responds and helps his people for his name sake.

And after hearing all of this from the Lord, it made me more motivated to help the little children, because I am telling you, they are the apple of the Lord's eye, and they are part of his present and they are going to be gift wrapped for him soon. These little kids, they love him and they do not have any other gods, because when you live in the garbage dump for years, what other god would you have? Are you going to pick another god out of the garbage? I do not think so.

THE LITTLE HEARTS ARE PRECIOUS TO HIM

Those little hearts are all his, and he loves them, and he has me working to help them, and other people are getting motivated to help them as well. And there are lots of little children out there, and there are lots of good ministries, but we need to be doing something for the Lord right now, and we need to be getting our lives straightened out with the Lord.

We need to check in with God because after the Lord talked with me about all the different types of gifts that he has received, I was astonished in my heart. I did not expect to get a message about how all of us had disappointed him so much. And the most amazing thing is it really hurt his feelings. People do not realize the Lord has feelings. Most people assume he spends eternity on his throne as he is pictured in the prophetic writings, as if he sitting on his throne throughout the ages, and all the angels are all worshiping him and they think that is all he did for the last two thousand years. That is not it. That is just a picture of how high and lifted up he is, but God has a life up there in heaven you know, God has a life and he wants to share it with his people. He is life and he is living his life in more profound ways that we can even imagine.

The Lord has greatly blessed me, for he speaks with me, particularly this last year. It reminds me a lot of my earlier years, especially the four years of my life which I call the "Age of Miracles" in which he spoke to me audibly virtually every day.

THINGS WHICH ARE HARD FOR HIM TO SEE

The other day I was talking with the Lord, and I said to him, "Lord there's nothing too hard for you is there, there's just nothing that is too hard for you. Lord you could do anything, anything at all, because there's nothing too hard for you, huh Lord." He answered "That is true, there is nothing too hard for me to do, but there are things that are hard for me to see." Isn't that intense? Doesn't it make sense though, for He has to watch all of this. He is seeing all of the things that are going on in this wicked and adulterous age. We could not even handle it; but he has to look at it, and it is hard for him. He told me it is hard for him, and that is why his judgment is going to be so severe. The wicked and the people of the earth have made this really hard on the Lord, because everything we do affects him.

This is his creation, and he loves his creation. He loves all the things that he has done. He loves all of his works, and his mercy is over his entire creation. Even when people mistreat the animals, it grieves the Lord. This whole corporate agribusiness, it is horrible; these industrialized feedlots, they are an animal Auschwitz, a corporate concentration camp. The suffering of his creation grieves the Lord; the suffering of his children and all of the evil, the corporate wars, the human trafficking, the murders, and the wounding of all the hearts, and the babies being slaughtered in their mother's womb. And the list just goes on, and the Lord is watching all of this. And he said "it is hard for me" and isn't that profound? All of this is hard on God. That is why he is so angry now. The Lord is furious, and the fires of his wrath are kindling even now before his face. "Behold, the day of the Lord comes, cruel both with wrath and fierce anger, to lay the land desolate: and he shall destroy the sinners thereof out of it."[98]

When God is watching us, we better not be making it hard on the Lord. We better be the people, that when the Lord is looking at us, he is being comforted by what he sees. He looks upon his saints, the ones whose hearts are true to him, and it comforts him; his faithful sons and daughters, they are all waiting for him, and they lift him up in their hearts, and it comforts the Lord, from all the bad things he has to see. We want to be the faithful servants who are waiting on the Lord. We do not want to be the people who grieve him, because we gave him our leftovers. How rude is that?

THE LORD GAVE US EVERYTHING

God gave us everything and all he asked of us is a first fruit offering and some of us would not even do that. Some of us would not even do anything at all. Think of yourself as a parent, and you are blessed with a lot of children, and you really are a wonderful parent, and you did everything for your children. You have given them everything that you could give, and some of them are so grateful. When they come to your house, they ask you is there anything we can do for you mom? And they bring a precious gift on every special day because they know how much you have done for them and they want to show you, they really are thankful and they appreciate you, and they love you so much. When it is appropriate, they buy you a really nice gift; they look really hard for the right one, something they know you would really value. Maybe it cost them a lot of money, but they saved up for it, because they wanted to show you how much you meant to them.

Then there is the child that forgets your birthday, and hardly ever shows up, and if they do bother to come and visit you on your special day, they only get you something they picked up on the way, as they were driving to your house, something left over. Maybe they picked up a card at the gas station on the way to your house, and they did not even bother to sign it. They are still your child, so you are not going to disown them, but if that goes on for a while, maybe some might forgive once or twice, but if that is the consistent recurring pattern, you are not going to be real happy eventually, are you?

No, you are not. And that is how some people have been with the Lord. They have insulted him. There are Christians who have offended God and is that not amazing. We have all sinned, and our sin is something we should all stop. We should have stopped sinning by now, and should be cleaning up the matters of our heart. We should not be dealing with any outward sin in our lives anymore, but some of us have not really honored the Lord.

Some of us have honored him a lot and it matters to him; the ones that have honored him, it touches his heart, and that is why he did this. When you really love someone, it feels a whole lot better if they love you back. It just works that way. Love does not last forever if it is just going in one direction. No, it will stop; you cannot have a relationship where one person is always giving, giving, giving, and the other person maybe sends a basket of rotten peaches once in a while after they eat the good ones themselves. That is going to really turn things around, isn't it?

Some of the people invited the Lord to Thanksgiving and then they told him "could you come on Friday? The house will be a little too crowded and we don't have room for you on Thursday." Some people even told him "could you use the maid's entrance on the side of the house because we really don't want our neighbor seeing you coming in the front door." The Lord is not happy when he is treated poorly by his people, and what King would be? Not a one. So that is a little taste of *The Present* message, which will be part of one of the next volumes.

IT IS BETTER TO GIVE THAN TO RECEIVE

It is all about the gifts we give, and the gifts we receive; and the gifts we give to each other, they matter to the Lord a whole lot.

Now maybe I am just preaching to myself, but we have to do a good job for the Lord, and we have got to show up and bring a present that is going to please him because he deserves it. He created us and then he died for us, in order to cover our sin. I had no idea what the cross was like, and none of us can really imagine what the Lord went through in the suffering that he endured for us.

Now the Lord is not asking us to be crucified for him, he is asking us to deny our flesh, which has caused all of the problems in our lives; and has never made anyone happy, and has never produced anything good. Let's get real here, what is God asking of us that is so hard? Give a first fruit offering, a tithe out of all the blessings with which he has blessed us?

And then he says in the word of God, if you do, he will bless your whole life, because the Lord turns right around and gives it back to you. He just wants us to learn to trust him, and he needs someone to help the poor, the widows and the orphans; and if you do, God turns right around and blesses you.

But many people do not bring a gift for the Lord, and many do not honor the Lord, but they do so to their own loss. Because the gifts that we receive in terms of the kingdom and in eternity are going to be as valuable as the gifts we have given to the Lord. God asked for the First Fruits, but some people threw themselves into the offering plate; they gave their entire lives to the Lord, for they love the Lord so much they could not just give ten percent, they wanted to give everything.

GOING ALL IN WITH THE LORD

There are people that went all in with the Lord. Then there are the people that did not go in at all, and these are going to receive nothing in return. And the people that went all in with Jesus, they are going to receive from the Lord everything. He is going to go all in with them. They were the wisest ones among us, and even the laborers who showed up in the eleventh hour get the same reward.

You can still go all in with Jesus, and you will still get the same reward. Some people went all in thirty years ago, and they are going to get everything, which means they are going to get the Lord as their reward. That is the gift they receive for having gone all in for God, and that is the gift they get for all of eternity. They are going to have a relationship with the Lord that not everyone is going to have.

Some did not have the faith to believe God, or they did not have the heart to really appreciate what Jesus did for us. Maybe they were just miserly men, who though holding onto their lives and all of their money would somehow be better for them, but they have played the part of the fool.

The Scripture says your wealth cannot deliver you in the day of the Lord's wrath. That money will become a curse, at this point that money is already cursed, and now the Lord is going to take it right out of your hands, so that it cannot profit you at all. You have already dishonored the Lord with it. How could you possibly think it would profit you? You must not understand how this works at all.

It is the same with our time. We hold our time back, we do not give any time to the Lord; we do not make any time for the Lord. What are we thinking? As if we are going to somehow be more productive if we cheat the Lord and we steal from God and we break his heart, because we never show up. Are you kidding? The Lord told me, "anybody who takes anything from me, I take it right back from them." You cannot steal anything from the Lord without God burning a hole in your pockets; and that includes anything you take from anyone else, because God counts it as all his. It is all his, so you cannot steal anything and keep it. It is all his anyway. We are the ones who are confused, because we think it is ours and it is not.

EVERYTHING IN THE EARTH IS MINE

I remember the Lord told me once that I was going to have a car accident, and he told me exactly where and when. I was driving with another believer and he spoke to both of us in an audible voice, and said "don't worry about the car, it will be just a little ding, and besides it's my car." I was really young at the time, and I did not know the Lord owned everything in the earth, so I said "Lord I thought this was my car." I was just being honest, and the Lord said to me "everything in the earth is mine including your car."

That was a new teaching for me. So I turned to my brother who was with me, and said "the Lord's going to crash his car, this is going to be really fun, we have to watch for the crash." We knew the location and I wish I had a video of this because it would be hilarious to watch as we were all scrunched down and in crash position bracing for impact, because we knew we were going to crash.

Well today, the United States is about to have a major accident, only this will be a really big crash and it will affect the whole country. It is not going to be a little ding this time; this one is going to total the whole car. Instead of a minor fender bender, this crash will also involve fatalities, many of them. This country will be so wrecked that it will simply end up in the junkyard; it is going to be towed away and you will never see it again.

If any of us think we are going to get through this time holding on to our American currency, while the really big money around the world is trying to get rid of the US dollar as fast as possible right now, and if we think our money is going to help us somehow, we are kidding ourselves. And if we think trying to hold onto our gold will help, we are also dreaming, because the Scripture says "their gold shall be removed."[99]

PEOPLE STILL DON'T BELIEVE HIM

The smartest thing any of us could do right now, is to help the poor and bless the widows and orphans within the kingdom of God, because the Lord says if you give to the poor, you are lending to him. God counts it is a loan. It is not even a gift. Look at how the Lord is trying to motivate people to help the poor and bless widows and orphans. He says "I am going to count it as a loan, and I will repay you." And yet the people do not believe him. They still think it is safer if they hold onto it themselves. I think they are dreaming. They are going to find out fairly quickly they were dreaming, because their gold is about to be removed.

"They shall cast their silver in the streets, and their gold shall be removed: their silver and their gold shall not be able to deliver them in the day of the wrath of the LORD: they shall not satisfy their souls, neither fill their bowels: because it is the stumbling block of their iniquity."[100]

Our silver and our gold cannot deliver us, rather it will be removed. At some point during the coming judgment the gold the people saved up for the last days, will literally be taken from them; it will be removed and they shall suffer a total loss, both in this world and in the next.

Had they given it to the Lord, to the help of the poor, the Lord promised to repay them. The Lord told me, he repays them twice; first in this world, and then again in the next. So holding on to our wealth, thinking that it is our strong tower for what is about to begin, we have deluded ourselves and we have robbed ourselves twice from all the blessings we could have walked in. So, in helping the poor, you actually get to double your money with God; but we would rather hold it in our grimy little hands, based on the hope or the dream, that it might somehow deliver us in the day of the Lord's wrath. Such is the thinking of fools, sailing on a ship of fools, and they are all truly lost at sea. And what will become of everything that we set aside, that each of us has reserved, for only me. You can add up that number and you can count it up high, because that is the measure of the losses that we will share, both you and I.

THE LORD COUNTS IT AS A LOAN

Alternatively, if we are wise enough to believe the Lord, and give help to the poor, then the Lord counts it as a loan. For some of us, we would be making up for some rather junky gifts we gave the Lord in the past, and for others who never even showed up at all, it might make the Lord feel a little better when he sees our name on his list.

In any event, giving to the poor is the only way to transfer the wealth of this world into eternity. You no doubt have heard it said, once you are dead, you cannot take anything with you, and you do not see a U-Haul behind any hearse. It is true, you cannot take anything with you, but you can send some things ahead of you. You can make some deposits into heavens bank account, where thieves cannot break in and were the rust cannot ruin, and you will have the good faith and credit of our beloved Lord promising you a just reward.

THE MONEY MATTERS

God's attitude in this money matter is very serious, because he understands how serious this whole matter of money really is. We work hard all of our lives to earn it, and it is real, it is not confetti, and it is not worthless paper, at least not yet. So, in giving to the poor, and in trusting the Lord, you are really putting your money where your faith is. God takes that as serious, because it is, and it is too bad the church did not use better wisdom, and avoid giving money to counterfeit Christian ministries, which burned up the majority of the tithes and offerings of the church for the last 30 to 40 years. While the real ministries all struggled, Satan was cunning enough to establish a bunch of counterfeit Christian ministries, then put them on television, and tell the people if you give your money there, God will make you rich. Nothing could have been further from the truth.

The Scripture says if you give your money to the rich it is a curse. These men were merely lying to you, and not a word they said was true. The Scripture also says if you give to the poor, you are lending to God. God didn't promise to make you rich, he merely promised to pay you back, and so in truth, your gift to the poor would cost you nothing. You would also be storing up riches for eternity; it would cost you nothing other than believing the Lord. But alas, most of us did not really believe the Lord.

IN THESE FINAL HOURS

So, in this final hour, before all of our American money becomes worthless, and before all of our gold is removed, and before the majority of us are reduced to the status of wandering refugees, we still have the opportunity to trust in the Lord, and to take God at his word, and give him a present that he will value, and a gift and an offering fit for a King. It is our choice and it is our life to lose. We can lose it, or we can give it to the Lord. We can give it to him, or we can try to save it for ourselves; each of us faces this decision within. Make your choices well brethren, for the days of vengeance shall soon begin.

God in his word commanded us to bring the First Fruits as our offerings from our harvest, and the First Fruits from our lives, and all he required was ten percent, which is really not much. It is a low income tax, a small tip on a restaurant bill, but it is all the Lord required and commanded of his people. If the truth be known, the tithe was not a tax at all, it was a test, to see if any understood the heart of the King, and to see if any would go and give beyond what was required. Would any perceive that these gifts were all being given back to the King who had already given us everything? It was just a test of our faith to reveal our love.

The Lord has given us everything, even all of his love. There is only a little sand left within the hourglass of heaven, a few sands of time to decide whether we will trust the King, one last time to bring him a worthy offering. You can still decide to keep what is yours. But do you believe you are going to save your life by what you keep for yourself? If you do, I do not want to be there to see what happens to you. But if you are willing to lose your life for Jesus sake, in the days which are ahead, I would be blessed to walk beside you.

"For thou, LORD, will bless the righteous; with favor will thou compass him as with a shield."[101]

The favor[102] of the Lord is given to those who are the delight of his heart, and to those who are found acceptable in his sight. For it is his good pleasure to give them the kingdom. And he counts them among his remnant in this hour.

The Prayers of the Remnant

Watch therefore, and pray always, that you may be accounted worthy to escape all these things that shall come to pass, and to stand before the Son of man. Luke 21:36

The First Fruit teaching originally came forth as a message on my Saturday evening blog talk program which I call *Search the Scriptures*. The teaching on the First Fruit Company began with this Holy Spirit inspired prayer:

Father, we bless you, for you have been so good to us. Father, you are always good, and your ways are always righteous and true. It is your will, and your purpose to lift up the name of your son, Jesus, for he alone is worthy of all glory, honor and praise. So, Father we come before you in Jesus' name. Father, we gather together in these final hours of the lives that we have all known, to hear your word of truth, and the sound of your trumpet, warning your remnant, and we thank you that you have warned your people, and also that you have revealed unto us, the plans of the enemy.

Father, we thank you, for in this day, which is your day, you also have a plan for your people and it is a good plan. It is a holy and a righteous plan, and it is your purpose that you would lift Jesus up in our hearts, and that we would all decrease in order that Jesus would increase in every one of us. Father, we all pray and we look to you in Jesus' name.

Lord Jesus, I offer thanksgiving to you. And may the people offer you the thanksgiving of praise out of pure hearts, that we would bless you. Lord, so many times we have come to seek your face, and call upon your name, for we have burdens on our hearts, and we need your help. Lord, we have needs, and concerns, and we desire your blessings and deliverance and Lord, we long for, and we wait for, your salvation. But tonight I want to come for you and I want to comfort you.

I WANT TO COMFORT YOU

Lord, we come for you tonight. Let us bless you. Let us bring joy to your heart and comfort you, for you have done so much for all of us. I pray that our hearts would be awakened and the eyes of our understanding would be opened that we could see clearly Lord, that you called us to minister to you, for your work is finished. Lord, you overcame this world, and by your death on the cross, our sins can be covered, and the doors to your temple are now open. So, tonight we repent of our sins. Forgive us for our ignorance and for the blindness of our hearts. Forgive us for the things we did not even know we were doing. Forgive us for our selfishness, our carnality and, Lord, for showing so little respect to you.

THE REMNANT ARE HIS PORTION

Lord, you should be first in our lives, and our hearts should bring you a First Fruit offering each and every day, for that is your portion and it is rightfully yours. Lord among those who are called to be your first fruit offering, we come bearing gifts in our hands, but we also place ourselves on the altar as an offering for you. Our lives are the gift we give to you, Lord. I pray that by your Holy Spirit you would bring us a word of truth tonight and that you would also bring forth truth from within our hearts, that you might accept us as your first fruit offering.

Lord, we need your mind tonight, and we need to hear the truth tonight. You also desire our praise and our love tonight, so I pray our hearts will be open, and that we would give unto you, that which is rightfully yours, and that we would present ourselves as living sacrifices, and would offer unto you an offering in holiness that would be well pleasing unto you, Lord, that you would not be grieved over the gifts that we bring. So many give you the leftovers of their lives, so many fruitless branches bear no fruit at all, while others bring gifts and the offerings which have spoiled. Lord, you have given your best to us and you put us first, even though you are God Almighty, in your great love for your people, Lord, you put us first. You came to serve and to tend to our needs and you gave everything for us, and held nothing back, and in so many ways we have defrauded you. Lord, forgive your people.

OPEN OUR EYES THAT WE MIGHT SEE

Lord Jesus, apply your salve to our eyes, that we might begin to see; awaken us from our sleep, that our hearts could become alive and awakened unto the Spirit, that we would come out of our Adamic sleep and that we could awaken unto righteousness, for you have called us for such time as this, to be the people that walk with you through the fires which are coming soon.

Lord, we are all about to go into the furnace of affliction, and the only way we are going to make it through is by walking with you. We are going to be walking on strange ground soon, and we are going to find ourselves in a strange place. Lord, you are about to begin your *strange work* and you are about to bring to pass your *strange act* among your people. You mean it for our good, for you are going to prepare your people for your wedding feast and you are going to have a people that are holy. You are going to have a bride that is spotless. There a present is going to be presented to you and it is going to be perfect. So Lord, let this word of truth be a blessing from you. Let this book minister life to your little flock, so that your saints may begin to offer you their hearts, in worship and adoration and in the love that you are due, for who you are, and for all you have done for us. For you have given us everything, for Lord, you have given us yourself.

LET US RESPOND IN RIGHTEOUSNESS

Let us respond in righteousness and let us respond in kind. Let us respond from a true heart and give everything unto you, for you are worthy Lord. None of us is worthy, apart from your grace and mercy; we would all perish in our sins. You paid an amazing price for our salvation. I do not know how you found the strength, but Lord your strength was in the power of your love. God, you love us more than we even know, and our love for you is so shallow. God, awaken us, that we could walk with you in the perfect covenant which you promised, in which we could become more than conquerors, overcoming the wickedness of this current dark age, separating and setting ourselves apart from this adulterous generation, to come out from Babylon, and from the deceptions and the darkness of this hour, and walk with you in the wondrous glory of your eternal light of truth.

Lord, I pray that a word of truth would come forth tonight. I yield the podium and this microphone to you, and I ask you to speak tonight, for I have nothing in me. I have spent all I had today laboring in your book. I bless you Lord, for the book you are about to bring forth for your people, because it is going to bring deliverance and victory, and it is going to crush the head of the serpent in the lives of many.

It is going to be like a pillar of righteousness thrown from the heavens to smash the kingdom of darkness. Lord, tonight, in the lives of the people that have gathered here together, let your word of truth break the head of the serpent. Let your truth set your people free; grant unto us true repentance, that we may present unto you offerings that are holy and righteous and true.

CONSECRATED UNTO YOU LORD

Lord Jesus, we consecrate this time to you, and we ask that you would speak. I could speak to the people for you, but it is always better if we hear from you. The people do not gather to hear me; they come to hear from you. And I need to hear from you as well, so Lord, we all bow before you in our hearts and we lift our hands and we say Holy, Holy, Holy is the Lord, and let all the earth declare your glory and praise and may you be blessed tonight.

Lord, let me minister to the people through the power of your Spirit that your word of truth would come forth, for the edification of your people. And unto me, who am among the least of your Saints, is this grace given, that you might show that the work was done by your hand, and that all the glory would be yours. So, you be glorified tonight Lord, and be blessed; we bless you Lord, we bless you and honor you, and we love you. Let your love shine in our hearts, more and more each day, unto the dawning of the perfect day that is coming so soon, as we look forward to the time with you, in your kingdom of eternity.

Between now and then, Lord, equip us to be profitable servants that we might work in your field, laboring with pure hearts, in the purposes for which you have created us, that you would be well pleased with us, and that you would be blessed. And we pray all of this in your name, Lord Jesus. Amen. Hallelujah. Hallelujah!

Thank you for taking the time to read the first volume of the *Search the Scripture* series. The second volume, *You shall know the Truth*, shall come forth shortly, for this matter of the King is urgent and of great importance, so that His servants could be warned and instructed, for the time of testing shall soon begin.

God bless you all.

Please remember me in your prayers

Benjamin Baruch

FOOTNOTES

[1] Jeremiah 7:29

[2] Micah 7:4

[3] Jeremiah 17:9

[4] Matthew 15:8-9

[5] Isaiah 1:9

[6] Very small - H4592, מעט, mᵉʿaṭ, a little or few: almost none, very few, lightly, little, very small, some, soon, X very.

[7] Isaiah 10:22-23

[8] Consumption H3617, כלה, kâlâh, a completion; adverbially completely; also destruction: - altogether, be, utterly consumed, consummation (-ption), was determined, a full, and utter end, riddance.

[9] Abomination H8441, תועבה תעבה, tôʿêbah, something disgusting (morally), an abhorrence; especially idolatry or an idol: abominable (custom, thing), abomination.

[10] Psalm 138:6

[11] Jeremiah 50:31-32

[12] 1Peter 4:1-2

[13] Suffer G3958, ðáó÷ù, pathos, to experience a sensation or impression (usually painful): feel, passion and to suffer, or to vex.

[14] 1ˢᵗ Peter 4:19

[15] Forgive G863, ȧöéçìé, aphiēmi, to cry, forgive, forsake, lay aside, leave, let it alone, omit, put away, remit, suffer, yield up or give it up.

[16] Matthew 6:14-15

[17] Trespass G3900, παράπτωμα, paraptōma, a side slip, a lapse or deviation, that is, an unintentional error or a willful transgression: - fall, fault, offence, sin, trespass.

[18] Genesis 6:5

[19] Heart, H3820, לב, lêb, the heart; the feelings, the will and even the intellect; the centre.

[20] Psalm 138:6

[21] Psalm 10:2

[22] Psalm 10:4

[23] Psalm 12:1-3

[24] Jeremiah 9:4

[25] Matthew 11:29

[26] Mark 7:6

[27] John 14:27

[28] Jeremiah 6:4

[29] Woe H188   אוי, ʾôy crying out; lamentation; Oh! alas, woe.

[30] Matthew 24:21

[31] Matthew 24:4

[32] Matthew 26:38

[33] Watch G1127, ãñçãïñåóù, gray-gor-yoo'-o, to keep awake, that is, watch (literally or figuratively): be vigilant, wake, be watchful.

[34] Mark 14:38

[35] Temptation G3986, putting to a proof (by experiment of good, experience of evil, solicitation, discipline or provocation); by implication adversity: temptation, to try.

[36] Mark 14:41

[37] Isaiah 28:21-22

[38] Strange work H2114, זוּר, zûr, turn aside; strange, profane; commit adultery: another place, fanner, go away, strange thing.

[39] Strange act H5237, נכרי, nok-ree', strange, (foreign, adulterous, different, wonderful): alien, foreigner, outlandish, stranger.
[40] Jeremiah 51:39-40

[41] Syncopation: Wikipedia, http://en.wikipedia.org/wiki/Syncopation

[42] Job 38:1-2

[43] Job 42:7

[44] Darkness H2822, חֹשֶׁךְ, chôshek, the dark; literally darkness; figuratively misery, destruction, death, ignorance, sorrow, wickedness: darkness, night, obscurity.

[45] Jeremiah 4:23

[46] Without form H8414, תֹּהוּ, tôhû, From an unused root meaning to lie waste; a desolation, figuratively a worthless thing; adverbially in vain: confusion, empty place, without form, nothing, thing of naught, vain, vanity, waste, wilderness.

[47] Void H922, בֹּהוּ, bôhû, From an unused root meaning to be empty; a vacuity, that is an undistinguishable ruin: emptiness, void.

[48] Knowledge H1847 דַּעַת, da'ath, dah'-ath, cunning, knowledge, awareness.

[49] Isaiah 27:7-9

[50] Afflicted H5221, נכה, nâkâh, to strike (lightly or severely, literally or figuratively): beat, give wounds, kill, punish, slaughter, smite, strike, be stricken, give stripes, surely wound.

[51] Isaiah 27:9

[52] Purged H3722, כּפר, kâphar, to cover; figuratively to placate or cancel: appease, make an atonement, cleanse, disannul, forgive, be merciful, pacify, pardon, to pitch, purge away, put off, make reconciliation.

[53] Isaiah 27:10

[54] Isaiah 27:11

[55] Isaiah 27:11

[56] Isaiah 27:11

[57] Isaiah 28:13

[58] Psalm 74:20

[59] Amos 8:12

[60] 2 Timothy 3:13

[61] Jeremiah 1:5

[62] Jeremiah 1:8

[63] Jeremiah 1:10

[64] Jeremiah 1:11-12

[65] Lamentations 3:1

[66] Man H1397 גבר, gheh'-ber, a valiant man or warrior; every one mighty.

[67] Arrows H1121, בֵּן, bên, a son

[68] 2 Chronicles 7:14

[69] Oates, Wayne, *Personality Disorders in Religious Behaviors*, Westminster Press, 1987

[70] Romans 7:24

[71] Psalm 119:165

[72] Proverbs 3:5

[73] 2Titus 3:13

[74] John 1:1-5

[75] Luke 11:34

[76] 2nd Corinthians 3:6-8

[77] John 1:6-7

[78] John 1:13

[79] John 1:14-17

[80] 2Corinthians 3:4-9

[81] Titus 3:9

[82] Romans 8:9

[83] Mark 16:17-18

[84] Ezekiel 34:2-4

[85] Ezekiel 22:25

[86] 2nd Corinthians 3:13-14

[87] 2nd Corinthians 3:16

[88] 2nd Corinthians 3:17

[89] Matthew 7:22

[90] Zechariah 13:2

[91] Jeremiah 10:14

[92] Jeremiah 10:15-16

[93] Isaiah 35:8-10

[94] www.blogtalkradio.com/dorothycrothers

[95] Psalm 12:6

[96] www.answerthecallinternational.org

[97] Isaiah 18:7

[98] Isaiah 13:9

[99] Ezekiel 7:19

[100] Ezekiel 7:19

[101] Psalm 5:12

[102] Favor H7522 רצון רצן, râtsôn, to delight: be acceptable, favour, good pleasure.

Made in the USA
Middletown, DE
21 December 2015